ESP

Fact or Fiction?

Terry O'Neill, *Book Editor*

Daniel Leone, *President*
Bonnie Szumski, *Publisher*
Scott Barbour, *Managing Editor*

OPPOSING
VIEWPOINTS®
SERIES

GREENHAVEN
PRESS®

THOMSON
─────✶─────™
GALE

San Diego • Detroit • New York • San Francisco • Cleveland
New Haven, Conn. • Waterville, Maine • London • Munich

© 2003 by Greenhaven Press. Greenhaven Press is an imprint of The Gale Group, Inc., a division of Thomson Learning, Inc.

Greenhaven® and Thomson Learning™ are trademarks used herein under license.

For more information, contact
Greenhaven Press
27500 Drake Rd.
Farmington Hills, MI 48331-3535
Or you can visit our Internet site at http://www.gale.com

Cover credit: © Fortean Picture Library

LIBRARY OF CONGRESS CATALOGING-IN-PUBLICATION DATA

ESP / Terry O'Neill, book editor.
   p. cm. — (Fact or fiction?)
   Includes bibliographical references and index.
   ISBN 0-7377-1066-7 (lib. alk. paper) — ISBN 0-7377-1065-9 (pbk. : alk. paper)
      1. Extrasensory perception—Juvenile literature. [1. Extrasensory perception.]
   I. O'Neill, Terry, 1944– . II. Fact or fiction? (Greenhaven Press)
   BF1321 .E87   2003
   133.8—dc21
                                                                    2002073859

Printed in the United States of America

Contents

Foreword

"There are more things in heaven and earth, Horatio, than are dreamt of in your philosophy."
—William Shakespeare, *Hamlet*

"Extraordinary claims require extraordinary evidence."
—Carl Sagan, *The Demon-Haunted World*

Almost every one of us has experienced something that we thought seemed mysterious and unexplainable. For example, have you ever known that someone was going to call you just before the phone rang? Or perhaps you have had a dream about something that later came true. Some people think these occurrences are signs of the paranormal. Others explain them as merely coincidence.

As the examples above show, mysteries of the paranormal ("beyond the normal") are common. For example, most towns have at least one place where inhabitants believe ghosts live. People report seeing strange lights in the sky that they believe are the spaceships of visitors from other planets. And scientists have been working for decades to discover the truth about sightings of mysterious creatures like Bigfoot and the Loch Ness monster.

There are also mysteries of magic and miracles. The two often share a connection. Many forms of magical belief are tied to religious belief. For example, many of the rituals and beliefs of the voodoo religion are viewed by outsiders as magical practices. These include such things as the alleged Haitian voodoo practice of turning people into zombies (the walking dead).

There are mysteries of history—events and places that have been recorded in history but that we still have questions about today. For example, was the great King Arthur a real king or merely a legend? How, exactly, were the pyramids built? Historians continue to seek the answers to these questions.

Then, of course, there are mysteries of science. One such mystery is how humanity began. Although most scientists agree that it was through the long, slow process of evolution, not all scientists agree that indisputable proof has been found.

Subjects like these are fascinating, in part because we do not know the whole truth about them. They are mysteries. And they are controversial—people hold very strong and opposing views about them.

How we go about sifting through information on such topics is the subject of every book in the Greenhaven Press series Fact or Fiction? Each anthology includes articles that present the main ideas favoring and challenging a given topic. The editor collects such material from a variety of sources, including scientific research, eyewitness accounts, and government reports. In addition, a final chapter gives readers tools to analyze the articles they read. With these tools, readers can sift through the information presented in the articles by applying the methods of hypothetical reasoning. Examining these topics in this way adds a unique aspect to the Fact or Fiction? series. Hypothetical reasoning can be applied to any topic to allow a reader to become more analytical about the material he or she encounters. While such reasoning may not solve the mystery of who is right or who is wrong, it can help the reader separate valid from invalid evidence relating to all topics and can be especially helpful in analyzing material where people disagree.

Introduction

Dale E. Graff was an aerospace engineer and physicist when he became a manager for a research program that involved studying and experimenting with remote viewing, in which a person uses extrasensory perception (ESP) to "see" a faraway place. The program aimed to discover whether remote viewing could be used in military intelligence gathering—specifically, spying. Graff believed in the program's potential, but he had no experience with remote viewing himself, and in spite of his optimism, he had some doubts. Therefore, one of the first things he did when he joined the program was set up a test to see if remote viewing could possibly work.

Russell Targ and Harold Puthoff, Graff's colleagues and conductors of the research, put him in contact with a remote viewer named Hella Hammid, who was in New York City at the time. Without saying where they were going, Graff drove the two men to the Ohio caves, a natural attraction thirty-five miles from Columbus—and about six hundred miles from Hammid. The three men toured the great caverns. Then, at an appointed time, Graff called Hammid and asked what she had "seen." She replied,

> This is strange. . . . I don't know what you guys got yourself into. It sure is scary! I saw . . . a maze of caves . . . brightly lit. You were in a misty place . . . deep underground. . . . At first I saw something like a wine cellar entrance, and an archway with wisteria, leading to an underground world. Then I saw caves, or mines . . . deep shafts . . . an earthy smell . . . moist passages. Silent, not much sound . . . scary . . . a golden glow all over. Only a few people. A very special place.[1]

Graff was stunned by Hammid's response. He had not dreamed that someone so far away could so accurately "see" what he was experiencing. This amazing incident confirmed Graff's belief that ESP was real. He started his new job with confidence that the research program would succeed.

But was this incident really an example of ESP? Graff would say yes, but most mainstream scientists would say that, if investigated, a more mundane explanation could be found. Most likely, they would say, Graff unconsciously gave Hammid clues that provided her "vision" of the caves.

What Is ESP?

Extrasensory perception is a relatively new term for a very old phenomenon: the supposed ability of some people to communicate with others and perform certain tasks through mental power alone. The term *ESP* was coined by researcher J.B. Rhine in 1934, but belief in the phenomena probably has been around since the beginning of human history.

ESP includes various kinds of phenomena, related by their seemingly supernatural ability to obtain or send information or cause things to happen without the use of the normal five senses of hearing, sight, smell, taste, and touch; it is an extra sense, often called "the sixth sense." ESP phenomena are also called *psychic* or *psi* phenomena. ESP phenomena can be divided into two basic categories. The first category involves receiving and sending information without the use of the normal senses. This category includes telepathy, remote viewing, precognition, clairvoyance, clairaudience, and other related phenomena. The second category involves the ability to affect objects or organisms by using mental energy. This is called *telekinesis*. Scientists who study these and other paranormal ("beyond the normal") phenomena are called parapsychologists. People who have ESP abilities, particularly of the telepathic or precognitive type, are often called psychics.

Telepathy is the ability to receive or send messages from mind to mind. Some call the ability to receive such messages mind reading. Remote viewing is the ability to "see" something that the eye is blocked from seeing—by walls or distance, for example. Precognition is the ability to know something before it happens. Clairvoyance is the ability to see something or to perceive something not visible to normal eyesight; remote viewing and precognition are forms of clairvoyance. Clairaudience is the ability to "hear" something unhearable by the ear—spirit voices or the words (or thoughts) of someone in a different location, for instance.

Some 80 percent of people say they have had some experience with or a belief in ESP, but mainstream scientists say that no clear evidence proves that ESP is real. They point to other explanations for most alleged ESP occurrences.

ESP in Action

Numerous examples of people's belief in ESP are found throughout history. Probably the most common example is belief in precognition. People of all times have routinely consulted oracles, prophets, witch doctors, psychics, and fortune-tellers to learn what the future will bring. People may believe these seers simply have the gift of seeing the future (precognition) or that they consult gods or spirits to gain their special knowledge.

Many ordinary individuals feel that they have forecast the future on a rare occasion, through a dream or a specially strong hunch, for example. Mark Twain, one of America's most famous nineteenth-century writers, described several of his prophetic dreams, including one foretelling his brother's death. Abraham Lincoln was said to have had a dream foretelling his own death. Television actress Lindsay Wagner had a feeling that she should not take a certain airplane in 1979. She was glad she followed her hunch because the plane crashed, killing all aboard. In a much lighter vein, many people report knowing who is calling them when the phone rings, even though they have no reason to expect a call from that person.

Much more unusual are incidents of telekenesis. Nineteenth-century travelers to India were amazed by the feats of fakirs, holy beggars who earned their living by performing mystical stunts. Fakirs were famous for the Indian rope trick, in which they supposedly used mental power to cause an ordinary rope to uncurl from a pile on the ground and gradually rise into the air like a snake uncoiling and becoming erect. Sometimes a person would climb up the rope, disappear at the top, and reappear again. Fakirs also lay on beds of nails without bleeding. Today, we know that many of these feats are tricks, but some are not easily explained.

During the 1970s a young man named Uri Geller came to the world's attention because of his alleged telekinetic powers. Geller started his career as a stage magician, but he quickly convinced many people that he could use his mental powers to bend spoons and keys, stop clocks, and perform many other amazing stunts. He even performed such feats on television—affecting the television viewers' watches, spoons, and other belongings! Geller was so convincing that scientists studied him, and some concluded that Geller's powers were real, though others did not agree.

Another example of telekinesis is the supposed ability of some people, called psychic healers, to use their mental powers to heal the sick and injured.

The Scientific Study of ESP

In some cultures ESP and other paranormal phenomena are simply accepted as a normal part of life. But in most modern societies, science and pragmatic thinking dominate, and people want to discover the scientific explanation for such things, or at least discover whether science can prove that these phenomena exist even though they cannot yet be fully explained. Several organizations have devoted themselves to the scientific study of such phenomena.

In 1882 the Society for Psychical Research (SPR) was established in London. The organization's members included scientists and prominent Londoners interested in the paranormal. The SPR was founded with the hope of scientifically proving that an afterlife exists and that it is possible to communicate with the dead. However, the organization also dedicated itself to studying all kinds of paranormal phenomena, including hypnotism (which was thought to be paranormal at the time), hauntings, and "thought transference" (ESP). In 1885 a similar organization was founded in the United States. The American Society for Psychical Research (ASPR) was briefly affiliated with the SPR but has been independent for most of its history. Both organizations continue to promote the scientific study of paranormal phenomena today.

During their early periods, these organizations were primarily concerned with "mediums"—people who claim to be in contact with the dead. But the SPR also conducted detailed surveys of people who claimed to have various kinds of paranormal experiences. The data from these surveys provided useful clues to researchers trying to learn more about ESP.

ESP was also studied by other peolpe and organizations. For example, in 1930 American novelist Upton Sinclair published *Mental Radio*, a book recounting experiments conducted with his wife, Mary. The book describes Mary Sinclair's ability to accurately reproduce drawings made by a person located in another room or even in another location several miles away.

J.B. Rhine and the Duke Studies

At about the same time, a young psychology researcher named J.B. Rhine and his wife, Louisa, set up shop at Duke University in Durham, North Carolina. J.B. Rhine established laboratory methods for studying ESP; Louisa Rhine collected and analyzed thousands of anecdotal accounts of spontaneous paranormal occurrences.

J.B. Rhine's laboratory work with ESP was unprecedented. He attempted to use rigorous scientific methods, and he claimed to find positive results. Many of Rhine's experiments involved statistical analysis of the results of guessing tasks. Many involved the use of a special set of cards called Zener cards. This is a set of twenty-five cards, blank on one side and containing a symbol on the other. The set includes five cards each of five symbols: a square, a circle, a star, a cross, and three parallel wavy lines. Rhine used the Zener cards to avoid the associations with standard cards (as with the queen of spades, the ace of hearts, and so on) that might influence the guesser's choices. A typical guessing task might have the guesser predicting which card would be turned over next. The guess would be recorded, the card would be turned over, and after a certain number of runs through the deck, the results would be analyzed statistically to determine if the guesser had a higher-than-normal guessing rate, which might indicate ESP (precognition).

Some experiments tested mind-to-mind ESP (telepathy). These involved a "sender" and a "receiver." The sender would turn over a card and send a mental image of it to the receiver. The receiver, who could not see the sender or the cards, would guess which card was turned over. Again, the results would be analyzed statistically.

Rhine also conducted telekinesis experiments. A typical experiment involved dice. A die would be ejected from a container. The subject would attempt to use his or her mind to influence the way the die landed.

Tests like those described above form the basis for much of the ESP research being done today. However, modern laboratories have improved on Rhine's techniques by using computerized random event generators (REGs). REGs do just what their name says: They are computer programs that randomly generate an ESP target—perhaps a picture, a sound, or a card hand—for ESP experiment subjects to try to perceive or affect.

Rhine's experiments resulted in a significant amount of data supporting the existence of ESP. However, Rhine's research and methods have been called into question. It seems clear that experimental controls were not as tight as they might have been, and some of the results reported by at least one of Rhine's researchers might have been doctored to look more favorable. Although today much of J.B. Rhine's research data is not held in great esteem, his work unquestionably has influenced the direction of ESP research.

The Maimonides Dream Studies

Another type of ESP research was carried out at Maimonides Medical Center in New York City during the 1960s. Researchers Stanley Krippner, Montague Ullman, and Charles Honorton wanted to know whether a person could send a message into another person's dream. A sender would concentrate on a particular photograph and attempt to send a mental image of it to a receiver. The receiver would be sleeping in another room with electrodes attached to his or her body. The electrodes would indicate when the receiver was in stage 1 REM (rapid eye movement) sleep, the sleep stage during which dreams most often occur. At this time, the researchers would awaken the receiver and have him or her record dream details. The dream accounts would be compared with the image being "sent" to the receiver. This study had a few promising results, but other scientists have not been able to duplicate the successes, so mainstream scientists do not consider them strong evidence of ESP.

The Ganzfeld and Remote Viewing

During the 1970s Charles Honorton established the Ganzfeld approach to remote viewing. Honorton believed that if distractions were removed, a receiver would be more able to use ESP. *Ganzfeld* means "whole field." In ESP research, the Ganzfeld approach is to completely clear the subject's "field" (environment) of sensory input. The subject may be placed in a comfortable reclining chair in a soundproof room in which the only sound is white noise (a sort of mild staticky sound that neutralizes other sounds). The subject's sight is completely blocked by a cover, such as two Ping-Pong ball halves painted red and filled with cotton. This prevents even light changes, such as from a person walking in front of the subject, from reaching the subject's eyes.

In a remote viewing telepathy experiment, a sender in another soundproof room concentrates on a randomly chosen picture, attempting to send it to the receiver. At the end of a specified time, the receiver is shown several pictures and is asked to select the one that was sent. Because the sender is in another room, and sometimes in another building, the receiver is considered to be attempting remote viewing, defined near the beginning of this chapter. The results are then tabulated and statistically analyzed.

During the 1980s, Ganzfeld experiments by Honorton and others showed a 35 percent success rate (compared to an expected 25 percent success rate by chance). Although results like these show promise, other scientists have had difficulty replicating the results, so they are not yet in agreement that Honorton's results are proof of ESP.

The Stanford Research Institute and the CIA

In 1970 Sheila Ostrander and Lynn Schroeder's book *Psychic Discoveries Behind the Iron Curtain* reported on the authors' travels throughout the Soviet Union (USSR) learning about the state of psychic research there. The book reports that the Soviet government was heavily involved in psychic research and believed it had substantial proof of various forms of ESP. This research, like so much else in the Soviet Union at the time, was kept secret from the Western countries until books and other reports like this one slowly began to expose it. The United States was understandably alarmed. It was the time of the Cold War, when the two superpowers— the United States and the USSR—were battling for world supremacy, though not in actual battles. The Cold War was waged mostly by subterfuge, with each side spying on the other, building nuclear strength, and cutting away at the other through strategic actions in countries allied with one nation or the other. The USSR's psychic discoveries were apparently being focused on potential war efforts: The Soviets were trying to find ways to use mind power to conquer their enemies.

Learning of Soviet psychic research, the United States quickly began its effort to catch up and established secret psychic research of its own. By 1972 the Central Intelligence Agency (CIA) was involved in full-scale experimentation with remote viewing, managed by the Stanford Research Institute, a Menlo, California, think tank funded largely by government contracts for various kinds of research. The remote viewing research went through several stages. First came simple in-house experiments in which the subject (remote viewer) would try to use ESP to discover what was inside a locked box, for example. Another stage had a sender at a remote location who would try to mentally transmit the sense of his or her own environment to the receiver. Another stage involved no sender; the receiver was simply given map coordinates and was told to send his or her mind to that location and report what was seen. One subject, artist Ingo Swann, supposedly remotely viewed the planet Jupiter and saw a ring surrounding it—before the spaceship *Pioneer 10* flew by the planet and photographed the ring that no one had previously known existed.

Ultimately, other U.S. agencies besides the CIA were involved in the research, which had many promising successes. But in 1995 the government called a halt to the research. The official statement indicated that the research did not have enough strategic value to continue funding.

Scientific Objections to ESP

Despite some seventy years of scientific research into ESP, mainstream scientists are not satisfied that any clear-cut evidence proves that ESP exists. In fact, one of the objections scientists have is that there seems to be no progress in ESP research. Each generation of ESP researchers may be able to discover a small amount of promising evidence, but they tend to prove the same thing over and over without breaking new ground or having a breakthrough to major findings. In other branches of science, small early discoveries build upon one another, constantly making breakthroughs to new levels of understanding. For example, several decades ago scientists were just beginning to understand atoms, which were believed to be the smallest units of matter. Then they discovered that atoms had smaller particles inside them—electrons and neutrons—and that these particles could be manipulated to produce massive amounts of energy. More research discovered even smaller particles and even more ways to use them. Scientists complain that similar progress has not been made in the field of ESP research. Scientists have other objections as well, some of which follow.

Anecdotal evidence. Much evidence for ESP is anecdotal—that is, it is from stories people tell about their experiences, but there is no way to scientifically evaluate these stories or replicate them. For example, a lot of ESP evidence is along the lines of a person saying they had a premonition that a relative was going to die, that a plane was going to crash, or that a certain person was going to win an election. But too often these premonitions are not recorded in advance, so there is no proof that the premonition actually occurred. And there is no way scientists can test to see if the person can make such a prediction again.

Reinterpretation. Sometimes people reinterpret the evidence to fit an ESP explanation. For example, psychics often get publicity when they use their ESP abilities to help the police solve crimes. But skeptics accuse many of them of providing vague clues and then reinterpreting the results. For example, psychics may tell the police that they "see" a murder victim's body near water and woods. First of all, this description could describe just about anyplace. Secondly, it is not surprising when a missing body turns up in woods near water. But if the body is discovered in a basement that has water pipes and wooden doors, the psychic's clues can be reinterpreted to mean this as well.

Inadequate experimental controls. In 1978 several scientists were conducting major studies of ESP in university laboratories. Professional stage magician James Randi was skeptical of the ESP research and believed that most of the scientists studying it were out of their league. They were not adequately controlling their experiments, and they were predisposed to believe in ESP. Thus, they were vulnerable to possible trickery. Randi arranged for two young men, experienced with some basic magician techniques, to be subjects in a program at Washington University in St. Louis, Missouri. Scientists studied the two young men for 160 hours over the next three years. According to Randi, the young men, allegedly using ESP,

> produced "spirit" photos on Polaroid film; bent spoons, keys, and coat-hangers; turned tiny propellers inside bell-jars; moved objects around on a table; traced cryptic messages in ground coffee sealed in an upturned fish tank; caused ghostly inscriptions to appear on paper sealed in glass jars; and in general convinced the researchers that they were bundles of psychic energy. . . . They did it by bullying the experimenters into doing things their way or not at all. The mice were running the experiments.[2]

The scientists were fooled and shared their amazing findings with colleagues. They were embarrassed when Randi exposed the hoax.

Randi's point in conducting this hoax was twofold: First, he wanted to prove that the experimental program was not sufficiently controlled, which is why the young men were able to get by with their tricks. And Randi did not believe the scientists at Washington University were unusually gullible; he believed inadequate controls were typical of such programs. Second, most scientists simply are naive when it comes to "paranormal" trickery. Randi believed that master magicians should be used as consultants for this type of research so that many types of fraud could be eliminated, putting the research on more sound footing.

Most mainstream scientists agree with Randi, particularly on point one. The major criticism they level against those who claim to have proven ESP in the laboratory is inadequate control: Experiments are not designed properly, monitored rigorously, or analyzed correctly.

Fraud. As Randi's example shows, ESP researchers can be fooled by hoaxters. There are all kinds of ways to fake ESP evidence. The article in chapter three of this book by Massimo Polidoro shows some ways that telekinesis can be faked, and the article by Ray Hyman describes a few of the ways that "mind readers" can fake ESP.

Test Your ESP

So, is ESP fact or fiction? Many parapsychologists believe that all people have ESP just waiting to be accessed, but other scientists say there is no such thing. Here is a way you can test yourself informally to see if you might have ESP. (A scientist would not consider this experiment controlled enough to be truly telling.) Take a deck of playing cards and shuffle them well, keeping them face down. Turn each card over, one at a time, but before you turn a card, predict whether it will be red or black. Keep track of how many hits and misses you have. A strictly average number of hits for a deck of fifty-two cards would be twenty-six. If you have several more hits, you might consider it suggestive of ESP—or perhaps you have "beginner's luck!" Try it several more times and see if your score changes.

Another explanation for an unusually good score, particularly if you have played with this deck of cards in the past, is that some of the cards might have subtle differences— nicks, bent corners, or other markings—that you unconsciously recognize.

If you would like to try additional ESP tests, go to this Internet page: www.gotpsi.org/bi/gotpsi.htm. These ESP test pages are maintained by the Boundary Institute, an organization that studies psychic phenomena.

Notes

1. Dale E. Graff, *Tracks in the Psychic Wilderness: An Exploration of Remote Viewing, ESP, Precognitive Dreaming, and Synchronicity.* Boston: Element Books, 1998, pp. 26–30.
2. James Randi, "The Role of Conjurers in Psi Research," in *A Skeptic's Handbook,* ed. Paul Kurtz. Buffalo, NY: Prometheus, 1985, p. 341.

Chapter 1

Fact or Fiction?

ESP Is Fact

Ted Serios: Psychic Photographer

Pauline Oehler

The mind can do some pretty amazing things, but can you imagine being able to take photographs merely by thinking? A Chicagoan named Ted Serios was said to be able to do just that. Serios would point an instant camera at himself, but instead of a self portrait, the camera would produce a photo of a place or object in a different location. This is called psychic photography, or "thoughtography," and it is a form of psychokinesis (the ability to affect objects by one's mind alone). Serios, the best-known "psychic photographer," has been extensively studied, in particular by Denver psychiatrist Jule Eisenbud, who is utterly convinced that Serios's powers are real.

Serios is not the first "thoughtographer," nor the last. However, he is probably the most thoroughly studied. He was poorly educated, shy, and an alcoholic, yet his photographs astonished many people. His psychic photography abilities were strongest during the 1950s and 1960s, but researchers have continued to work with him sporadically, often with amazing results.

Excerpted from *The Psychic Photography of Ted Serios*, by Pauline Oehler (Chicago: Society for Psychic Research, n.d.). Copyright © by Illinois Society for Psychic Research. Reprinted with permission.

21

The instant camera mentioned in this article—the Polaroid-Land camera—was the forerunner of today's instant cameras. The user would put a sealed film pack into the camera, pull out a bellows (an accordion-like part of the camera that moves the lens into the correct position for picture-taking), pull a paper tab out of a slot in the camera to unseal the film pack, and then push a button to take a photo as you would with any other camera. After each picture was taken, the user would pull another paper tab from the slot. The tab was attached to a chemical-filled, multilayered piece of blank film material. The user would rub a wet developing chemical over the film, then wait a specified period of time. Within moments a photograph would appear on the film.

The article's author also mentions spirit photography. This involves photos allegedly showing real spirits (ghosts). Spirit photography was particularly popular during the late 1800s and early 1900s.

At the time Pauline Oehler wrote this article, she was a member of the Illinois Society for Psychic Research, which sponsored some of the early research involving Ted Serios.

The world's most remarkable photographer may well be a humble and obscure Chicago man named Ted Serios. So far as is known, Mr. Serios is the only person in the world who can point a camera at his own head and catch a picture of the Chicago Natural History Museum. Incredible as it seems, he has done just that from a closed room in my home 15 miles from the scene, before witnesses, and with my Polaroid-Land camera fresh from the shop where it was checked and loaded from stock.

Mr. Serios has been taking his phenomenal photographs for the past eight years with a variety of cameras and film, in color and in black and white and, in one experiment, in motion. He has produced photographs of places he never has been, never has seen, and of which, so far as can be determined, he has no previous knowledge.

Present knowledge of the laws governing the physical universe cannot explain this phenomenon. Mr. Serios himself makes no attempt to. He is as mystified by his talent as is everyone else who has witnessed it.

Spirit Photography

"Spirit photography" is almost as old as photography itself. Extra faces and human forms have been making unexplained appearances on photographic plates and film since 1861. Caught in the cross-fire between Spiritualists and anti-Spiritualists, however, its claims have not been examined with scientific objectivity.

When phenomena are inexplicable by natural laws the possibility of fraud always looms large. When they also are incompatible with accepted theory the charge of fraud often proves a sanctuary too tempting to resist. This seems to have been the fate of "spirit photography." Although it persists in Spiritualist circles down to the present its validity never has been satisfactorily established.

It must be admitted, moreover, that considering the possibilities of the dark room the chances for fraud are considerable.

But psychic photography employing a Polaroid-Land camera is quite another matter. The simple precaution of providing one's own camera and film reduces the opportunity for trickery almost to zero.

Within the past few months Mr. Serios has demonstrated his psychic photography using the Polaroid-Land cameras provided by a number of scientists, photographers and other intelligent observers. There is no longer doubt among those who have witnessed these demonstrations. He does take the photographs. There is no trickery. And they are paranormal. . . .

Serios Demonstrates His Skills

The demonstration took place in the reception room of the suite of offices—a room without windows. The witnesses had watched a small Polaroid-Land camera loaded with a factory-sealed pack and had posed for a conventional shot of themselves for the first exposure of the roll.

The camera, ready for the second exposure, was handed to Mr. Serios who sat facing the witnesses in an armless, straight-backed chair against a blank wall. With the camera pointing at his upper torso and head, Mr. Serios concentrated for a minute or two, then snapped the shutter. The camera was taken from his hands and 10 seconds later a street scene was pried up, torn from the roll in the camera and the fixative applied.

Later, standing on the sidewalk on the southeast corner of Jackson Blvd. and State St., I was able to verify every stationary detail as the entrance of Lytton's store, the electric signs on the next building to the east across an alley, and a good portion of the street before them.

Mr. Serios later took another photograph of the same buildings but with two cars and an armored truck passing on the street. . . .

The first time I personally saw Mr. Serios take a psychic photograph was on May 21, 1962, in my home in Wilmette [Illinois]. Present also were my mother, Mrs. Marion Lorentzen; my husband, a former advertising executive and since his retirement on account of illness, the author of the book, *The Great Sioux Uprising*, widely praised for its thorough and accurate research; our two daughters 18 and 16, and David Techter, executive secretary of the Illinois Society for Psychic Research.

The Polaroid-Land 800 camera used on this occasion had been examined during the afternoon in the Camera Shop of Wilmette by the clerk who had sold it to me three years before. After thoroughly inspecting it, in the presence of a second witness, the clerk loaded it with 10-second film taken from stock, signed the "leader" of the film roll which would have to be withdrawn from the interior of the camera before the first picture could be made, and then sealed the camera with initialed tape. Signed statements to this effect by both the clerk and the witness are on file.

Mr. Techter and the four family members all inspected the intact seal, saw me break it, extend the bellows, adjust the focus to EV 11 at Mr. Serios' request, pull out the signed leader and hand the camera to Mr. Serios.

Immediately after the first successful shot, before he had moved from the chair or had any opportunity to dispose of any possible secret equipment, Mr. Serios complied with a request to remove his shirt for search, and patiently submitted to a further examination of his undershirt and upper torso toward which the camera had been pointed.

The room was lighted in its normal way by three 150-watt bulbs in as many table lamps, two of which were approximately eight feet on either side of Mr. Serios. He was at all times in fully lighted view. An automatic Wink-Light flashed for each exposure.

Serios's Accessories

For some reason he is unable to explain even to himself, Mr. Serios, a Catholic, was accustomed to hold a rosary in his hand when he took pictures. For some months he also had been holding a cylinder of cardboard, $7/8$ inch high and $3/4$ inch in diameter and fastened with friction tape. He placed this around the lens to prevent his fingers from inadvertently covering it when the shutter was sprung. He since has abandoned both objects.

For the two occasions which are being described he had covered the paper cylinder with transparent Scotch tape. The purpose, he said, was to forestall criticism that he might be slipping micro-film images into the cylinder. The precaution was unnecessary since a transparency held this close to the stock lens of the Polaroid-Land camera will not reproduce. However, the cylinder was duly examined before and after each session and retained for the record.

The first picture of this session was a dud: the print showed the photographer's own shirt-front, collar and tie and a black mist where his head should have been. The second shot is . . . a strange photomontage. The most immediately discernible feature is a brick or stone building, upper right, with three apertures, apparently doors. It appears to be a public building shot from an angle slightly above and some distance away. In the left foreground a closeup shot of a statuesque head with closed eyes is partly obscured by a hand and wrist in still closer perspective extending from it into the lower foreground of the picture. The hand is cupped in the same way Mr. Serios cups his left hand around his cardboard cylinder and the camera lens. . . .

Search for a Dinosaur

Sunday afternoon, June 10, Mr. Serios again came to our house. This time he announced his intention of taking a picture of a dinosaur in its native habitat to please David Techter. Mr. Techter is a paleontologist with the Chicago Natural History Museum. Present on this occasion beside Mr. Techter were my husband and myself. Sixteen-year-old Sioux, studying in another room, was called to see the museum shot while it was still wet from the fixative.

The session began about 5:00 o'clock in the afternoon in

full daylight augmented by two 150-watt bulbs and the Wink-Light. A third 150-watt lamp was lighted before the session ended at 7:00 o'clock. Since the draperies were not drawn across the windows, Mr. Serios this time sat on a couch, his back to the wall with the large unglassed oil painting and facing the east windows. He held the camera in such position that each exposure of the series normally would have shown a portion of the picture and frame, wall, pole-lamp and part of a door in the background—all on the west wall—as well as a good portion of his own upper torso.

It was not considered necessary to have the camera examined and sealed as on the previous occasion, since Mr. Serios had no access to it and it had been used between times for conventional pictures. Again the aperture was set at EV 11 at Mr. Serios' request because it seemed to have worked well in the past.

As before, the camera was in Mr. Serios' possession for only the few minutes before each shot.

During these preliminary minutes he places himself into a light hypnotic state. He gazes directly into the lens which is about two feet away from his eyes. He believes this is the best distance for obtaining successful pictures.

For each exposure he was seated facing us, holding the camera upright against his crossed knee, thumb and index finger of his left hand holding the cardboard cylinder against the lens, the rosary in his right hand, right index finger on the shutter lever. Each time, immediately after he clicked the shutter, I removed the camera from his hands and extracted the print from the camera in the prescribed manner.

The first shot of this session produced only a badly focused portrait of Mr. Serios and the dark mass of the oil painting with a section of its ornate white frame showing in the background. This was the last exposure on a roll already in the camera, so I reloaded with 10-second film bought by myself and still factory sealed.

Just before he seated himself to take this second shot, Mr. Serios became uneasy, saying he had a feeling we were being watched.

Peculiar Paranormal Photos

With a recent unsuccessful experimental session for the benefit of two FBI agents in mind, Mr. Techter and I teased him about "Russian spies." Somewhat abashed, Mr. Serios then seated himself. Reiterating his determination to catch a dinosaur, he snapped the second shot.

It shows a peculiar shape which has suggested to those who have seen it an elephant beginning to take form out of a misty background. But when the print is reversed, the brow, nose, eye sockets, one in shadow and the other aglow with a staring eye, of a "Russian spy" appears.

Admittedly, interpretation of such ambiguous photos is as subjective as a Rorschach [inkblot] test. Nevertheless, the point must be stressed: *irrespective of interpretation, even these shots seem proof of a paranormal occurrence.*

The present state of man's knowledge cannot account for even such ambiguous images replacing the objects orthodox photography should have revealed any more than it can account for the view of the Chicago Natural History Museum which was soon to follow.

The right half of shot three is almost normal. It reveals part of the photographer's shoulder, the door jamb and pole-lamp behind him. But on the left half of the print Mr. Serios is blotted out by lights and shadows which at first view conveyed no meaning. Later examination revealed them to be part of a street scene which an hour or so later imprinted itself on the ninth exposure.

With the fourth exposure we were all sure Mr. Serios was now on his target. Billowing clouds seem to be forming an animal, less dinosaur than giraffe, its body reminiscent of a paleontologist's bony reconstruction in a museum when the print is turned sideways. But re-examination a few hours later revealed that when held in its normal position it too suggests the street scene finally captured on the ninth exposure. Here it was just beginning to form, this time not on just half, but over the whole frame.

Yet, even after this discovery, the giraffe is still there, tantalizingly suggestive of two separate ideas both trying to take shape, as in the second shot of the abortive elephant and the spy. It is hard to avoid the suspicion that what is pictured here is the actual creative process of the human brain. Shots of this sort are a common feature of Mr. Serios' photography apparently, but until its significance was noted in this series such photographs had been discarded as failures.

The fifth shot was an occasion for rejoicing. It is an unmistakable photograph of the Chicago Natural History Museum.

Let me state again for the record: there was no picture of the museum in the room, not even in any book although a search was made through three or four in an attempt to confirm the identification. Chicago's Museum of Science and Industry is also similar in appearance to the museum in the picture, and Mr. Techter, who has passed back and forth between those pillars every working day for some years, couldn't be sure they were four in number. But a photograph found in a book on an upper floor of the house verified the identification and the number of columns, thereby proving once again that the camera doesn't lie—not even when it is under the strange influence of Mr. Serios. . . .

The Opinion of a Camera Expert

By what means could these pictures have been fraudulently produced? The matter is considered in detail by Stanford

Calderwood. Vice President of the Polaroid Corporation in a recent letter to Curtis Fuller, President of the ISPR [Illinois Society for Psychic Research] and publisher of *Fate* [magazine]. In concluding Mr. Calderwood says:

> Let me stress that while a clever man could tamper in advance with our film, I know of no way he could do it if you were to show up with the film you bought in a store at random and watched him load and shoot. Tampering with the film would be a long and complicated procedure and nothing that could be done by sleight-of-hand especially if he had to photograph two or three pictures (or thoughts) on the same roll without reloading the camera and without an opportunity to substitute something in front of or behind the lens.

If my veracity is accepted, every possibility for fraud envisioned by Mr. Calderwood with the exception of the possible substitution of something in front of the lens is eliminated. In support of the accuracy of my report there is the concurrence of the witnesses.

The camera had not been tampered with beforehand; Mr. Serios did not open it nor handle it at any time when it was opened to remove the print or to replace the film. Hence he did not tamper with the film nor put a transparency behind the lens.

The only possibility for fraud that remains, therefore, is that he photographed something he placed *before* the lens.

If it is conceded that we observed correctly, photographs on the wall or any place in the room or attached to Mr. Serios' person will have to be eliminated. There were none.

Could he have concealed a transparency between his fingers? Mr. Serios is not a sleight-of-hand artist and he was being watched very closely; however, the possibility must be considered. Presumably he could conceal a transparency no larger than a thumb nail. What could he do with it?

The Polaroid-Land 800 is equipped with a rather simple

lens. There is no way it could blow up a transparency of such size to cover the $3\frac{1}{4} \times 4$ inch area of the print. There is no way Mr. Serios could reproduce a transparency with this lens to cover the area of the print unless it were three or four feet from the camera and its dimensions ran into feet, not inches.

To produce such a picture he would have to have a wide-angle lens of very high diopter (refractive power). It would have to be especially ground. It could not be framed and clamped onto the regular lens without being obvious.

But he had his cardboard gadget in front of the lens. Let us assume it did not have the innocent purpose he claimed but was instead the means by which he held the special lens in place. Only his right hand was available. The left hand, with the rosary, was on the shutter lever and could not be utilized for holding anything in front of the lens.

Mr. Serios held the cardboard cylinder with only thumb and forefinger. The other fingers of his right hand were *behind* the lens. He had only the two digits which must hold the cylinder and press the special lens against the fixed lens.

Where would he hold the transparency he is to photograph?

And with what?

He cannot press it directly on the lens with the cardboard cylinder, for at this range it will not reproduce. With the highest possible diopter lens the transparency would have to be at least an inch away. And it was impossible for him to place a transparency at this distance without detection even if he had an extra thumb and forefinger on his right hand.

Scientists Have Proven the Ability of Russian Psychics

Sheila Ostrander and Lynn Schroeder

During the 1960s and 1970s persistent rumors originated from the Soviet Union (USSR) about scientific research being done with ESP and other paranormal phenomena. In the Western nations, paranormal phenomena, including ESP, were largely considered silly and impossible. But when word began leaking out about Soviet research involving these topics, and particularly when the rumors indicated that the Soviets were working on ways to use ESP and related phenomena for military purposes, Western authorities became interested.

However, at that time relations between the USSR and the Western countries, including the United States, were extremely strained. The Cold War was on, and the USSR and the Western nations were mutually suspicious and uncooperative, with both factions fearing that the other would start a nuclear war and try to conquer the other. Whereas West-

ern science prided itself on the open exchange of information—except where defense and weaponry were involved—
the Soviet Union kept information about all of its research
highly secret. But as Soviet scientists defected to the West,
and with the fall of the Soviet Union in 1991, detailed information about the Soviet research became available.

The following article reports on research done with one
remarkable woman, Nelya Mikhailova (also known as Nina
Kulagina). An ordinary middle-aged housewife, Mikhailova
was said to have amazing powers of psychokinesis (PK), the
ability to affect objects through mental power. Her abilities
were so strong that a 1968 Associated Press article said,
"When Nelya Mikhailova wants something, she just stares
at it and the object begins to creep toward her." The authors,
Sheila Ostrander and Lynn Schroeder, have written several
books about ESP and related phenomena. They traveled extensively in Russia and eastern Europe investigating the psychic research conducted there.

The story of Nelya Mikhailova the PK medium is excep-
tional and bizarre and, much more than the story of any
other psychic in Russia, exemplifies the political turmoil
and shadowy machinations that can sweep Soviet parapsychology and Soviet science. We were scheduled to see scientific films of the amazing Nelya in action the first day of the
conference in the "House of Peace and Friendship," a
miniature castle of studded stone and candy-cane columns
near a glassy new Moscow business district. . . .

Recent news reports had said Nelya Mikhailova (Mik-hil-
ova) could "command" bread, matches, cigarettes, or apples
to jump off a table. According to Soviet scientists her PK
power (ability to move matter at a distance) had moved and

stopped the pendulum of a wall clock, moved plastic cases, water pitchers weighing a pound, and an assortment of dishes, cups, and glasses. And all without touching the objects. Along with the scientists, reporters from *Moscow Komsomol* and *Moscow Pravda*, published by the city's Communist Party organization, said they'd watched the forty-one-year-old Nelya in action and found "no hidden threads, magnets, or other gimmicks."

Even more extraordinary, the list of scientists investigating Mikhailova read like a Who's Who of Soviet science. Chairman of Theoretical Physics at the prestigious Moscow University and holder of the Laureate of the State Prize, Dr. Ya. Terletsky publicly proclaimed on March 17, 1968, in *Moscow Pravda*, "Mrs. Mikhailova displays a new and unknown form of energy."

Physicists from the Soviet Union's Joint Nuclear Research Institute at Dubna had tested Mikhailova, as had those from the Institute of Physics of the Academy of Sciences of the U.S.S.R. The list included Nobel-prize winners. The Mendeleyev Institute of Metrology also studied Nelya and stated in *Moscow Pravda* that she had moved aluminum pipes and matches under the strictest test conditions, including observation on closed-circuit television. They could give no explanation of "the phenomena of the movement of objects.". . .

Mikhailova on Film

The film projectors churned and at long last we viewed the elusive Mikhailova PK film. Far from the *Pravda* portrait of Mrs. Mikhailova, which placed her somewhere between the Devil's consort and a Baba Yaga witch (the sorceress famous in Russian fairy tales), we saw on the screen a plump, attractive, open-faced young woman with dark, expressive eyes. She could almost have been a relative of cosmonaut

Yuri Gagarin, with her typically Slavic features—high cheek-bones and turned-up nose. Her dark hair was pulled back into a chignon and she wore a sleeveless lace blouse and plain skirt.

The experiments were taking place in Nelya's new apartment in a startlingly modern, brand-new district on the edge of Leningrad. This district was once part of the front line she had defended during the war. . . .

Mrs. Mikhailova was seated at a large, round, white table in front of a lace-curtained window. The Russians said she had already been physically examined by a medical doctor, who had even had her x-rayed to make sure there were no hidden objects or magnets concealed on her person, nor any fragments of shrapnel lodged in her body from her war injury. He found none.

The five-man film crew, scientists, and reporters moved in closer. [Biologist and Soviet parapsychologist Edward] Naumov placed on the table in front of Nelya a compass on a wristband, a vertical cigarette, a pen top, a small metal cylinder like a saltshaker, and a matchbox picturing a lunar spaceship—a figurative version of outer space confronting "inner space." The objects gleamed against the pale table like a still life by Dalí, poised on the edge of the supernatural.

Mikhailova's dark eyes concentrated on the compass—the easiest object to warm up on. PK is easier with rotating objects, say Western researchers. With clocks and compasses there's no static friction.

It sometimes takes Mikhailova two to four hours to rev up her supernormal powers, Naumov mentioned in his commentary as we watched the silent film. Nelya held her long fingers parallel to the table about six inches above the compass and began to move her hands in a circular motion. The strain etched the dimples deep in her cheeks. Twenty minutes passed. Her pulse raced to 250 beats a minute. She moved her head from side to side gazing intently at the compass needle. Her hands moved as though she were conducting some unseen orchestra. And then, as if the atoms in the compass needle were tuned in to her, the needle shivered. Slowly it began to spin counterclockwise, turning like the second hand of a clock. Then the entire compass, plastic case, leather strap, and all, began to whirl.

As the entire compass spun like a carousel, the lines under Mikhailova's eyes darkened and the wrinkles on her forehead deepened with the intense strain. She fell back exhausted.

"How much power she has depends on weather conditions, too," Naumov told us. "Her PK power diminishes in stormy weather."

Moving Matches and More

In the film, Naumov scattered a whole boxful of matches on the table, a foot or so away from Nelya. He placed a small nonmagnetic metal cylinder and a matchbox near them.

"She is selective," said Naumov. "She can move one or two objects from the group." Again Mikhailova circled her hands above the objects. She shook with the strain. Under her gaze the whole group of matches moved like a log-run on a fast-flowing river of energy. Nearby the metal cylinder also moved. Still interlaced like a raft, the matches went to the edge of the table and fell off one by one to the floor. Naumov put another batch of matches and a nonmagnetic metal case inside a large Plexiglas cube. The cube was to rule out drafts of air, threads, or wires. Mikhailova's hands moved a few inches from the Plexiglas cover and the objects shuttled from side to side of the plastic container. Whatever this energy was, it could easily penetrate Plexiglas.

Again Mikhailova looked drained. She had lost over three pounds during this half hour. It was as if she were converting the substance of her own body into energy. Many Western mediums also had reported this weight loss during PK.

"She was actually much sicker than she looked in the film," Naumov told us later. "The strain on her heart was so great we had to stop the cameras several times. It took us over seven hours to make the film and afterward she temporarily couldn't speak or see. For days after doing these tests, her arms and legs pained, she felt dizzy and couldn't sleep."

Was Mikhailova genuine or a "mystification," as the Soviet skeptics called it? From what we'd seen so far, PK was taking place under good conditions with competent observers present. It was no amateur home movie, but a costly 35-mm professionally-produced film, photographed by skilled technicians.

We recalled Soviet writer Lev Kolodny's recent visit to Mikhailova's apartment. He was busily writing down notes during an interview when, glancing up, he suddenly observed the top of his fountain pen creeping over the lace tablecloth toward him. "A lump stuck in my throat," he said. The top seemed almost to glide above the uneven surface of the lace. His hostess Mikhailova smiled as a glass tumbler also crept along behind Kolodny's pen top. "Both objects moved to the edge of the table as if they were in harness. The tablecloth wasn't moving—the other glasses beside mine were still sitting there. Could she somehow be blowing on them to make them move? There was no draft of cold air and Mikhailova wasn't breathing heavily. Why didn't a jar in their path also move? I ran my hands through the space between Mikhailova and the table. No threads or wires. If she was using magnets they wouldn't work on glass."

Kolodny picked up both moving objects, examined them, felt them all over, hoping to find some clue. Absent-mindedly, he put the glass over his pen top to form a dome. Mikhailova seemed to be intrigued with this arrangement.

She glanced at the pen top as she sipped tea. The top of the pen sped from side to side underneath the glass.

Mysterious Energy

"What kind of energy could have caused this motion, and what laws does it work on?" Kolodny wondered.

Of all psychic happenings in life, PK or telekinesis, as it is sometimes called, can be one of the eeriest. Spontaneous movements of objects generally happen at moments of crisis in a person's life. The grandfather clock that "stopped short, never to go again, when the old man died" has been recorded in song. Telepathy doesn't arouse the same shock as suddenly observing a table following you across the room.

How does Mikhailova manage to live with events like these happening around her all the time? "I didn't know until a few years ago that I could move things at a distance," she says. "I was very upset and angry that day. I was walking toward a cupboard in my apartment when suddenly a pitcher in the cupboard moved to the edge of the shelf, fell, and smashed to bits."

"After that, all kinds of changes began to take place in my apartment," she says. Objects seemed somehow to be "attracted" to her, as if the inanimate had become animate. It was almost like having a poltergeist in her home. Usually, scientists say, poltergeist activities are caused unconsciously by a young person in a household—generally at the age of puberty. Objects seem to move of their own volition— doors open and close, lights go on and off by themselves, the laws of gravity seem to be reversed.

But unlike most people plagued by a poltergeist, Nelya suddenly realized the "force" was coming from her. She discovered she could control this energy. She could make it happen by wanting it to. She could summon and focus this extraordinary energy at will. At home with her family, holding her grandchild in her arms, she made a distant toy move closer. While a friend gave her a manicure, she made a bottle of nail polish move without touching it with her polish-wet hands. The family dog, too, watched with bewilderment as objects near his mistress began to gyrate. Her fascinated husband made a home movie of her strange powers of PK.

"I think I inherited this telekinetic ability from my mother," says Mikhailova. "I also passed it on to my son."

Playing with Food

Often as we sat waiting in Soviet restaurants, we thought longingly of Mikhailova's purported ability to sit down at a table and have "dinner" jump toward her.

Soviet writer Vadim Marin, who is connected with the Popov research group, described it: "Mrs. Mikhailova was sitting at a dinner table. A piece of bread lay on the table some distance from her. Mikhailova, concentrating, looked at it attentively. A minute passed, then another . . . and the piece of bread began to move. It moved by jerks. Toward the edge of the table, it moved more smoothly and rapidly. Mikhailova bent her head down, opened her mouth, and, just as in the fairy tale, the bread itself (excuse me but I have no other words for it) jumped into her mouth!"

"I wasn't hypnotized," he added reassuringly. "It's all on film."

PK was affecting organic matter. Could PK also affect chromosomes or DNA or human tissue? One physicist told us Nelya could cause third-degree burns on her stomach by PK. In this line, researchers in the West have already found that under strict test conditions, psychics could influence enzyme and bacterial activity.

In the same film, Mrs. Mikhailova also is supposed to have moved simultaneously five vertical cigarettes that the scientists placed under a bell jar. Afterward the cigarettes were shredded to ensure nothing was secreted inside.

But what about the human being who was doing the influencing? What were his or her reactions during PK? With no instruments to measure PK, researchers could only file eyewitness accounts and occasionally infrared films of talented PK mediums like Eusapia Palladino or Rudi Schneider. "Fraud squads" of skeptics almost physically dismantled these mediums to search for magic tricks. The scientists, instead of thinking PK might take place under *certain* "human conditions" just as different laws apply in outer-space conditions, rejected PK out of hand.

Measuring the Biological Field

A group of Soviet scientists took up the challenge of studying PK in the human being. If Nelya Mikhailova was not a fraud and was really beaming some unknown energy at those objects on the table, what was happening inside her? What was happening around her?

Dr. Genady Sergeyev of the A.A. Uktomskii Physiological Institute (a Leningrad military lab) mulled over the problem. Psychokinesis implied action of the mind at a distance. Could a detector at a distance from the medium pick up traces of this PK energy, this uncharted human potential?

In Leningrad Dr. Sergeyev wondered if the human force field had anything to do with PK. The mind could directly influence this cocoon of energy around our bodies. Could he find a way to measure these biological fields and the mind's impact on them *at a distance* around Nelya?

Sergeyev came up with a new invention, a detector that picks up "biological fields" (electrostatic and magnetic) about four yards away from the human body without any direct contact. We saw the graphs made by these detectors in a film, but we were told the construction of the detectors was "not public."

Sergeyev put his new detecting devices to work measuring Mikhailova's force field while she was resting. He found the electromagnetic field constantly around her body is only ten times less than the 0.6 gauss of the magnetic field of the earth itself. The electromagnetic force field around Nelya is much stronger than average, says Sergeyev. The Leningrad Institute of Metrology also found this increased magnetic field around her body.

Dr. Sergeyev, an intense, solidly built man in his forties, was the only Russian to discuss his research that second day of the conference. Sergeyev's own "force field" radiated seriousness as he spoke. A former radio man in the Baltic during the war, the mathematician, also trained in neurophysiology, was obviously held in very high esteem by his colleagues. "He has done brilliant work," a Czech scientist told us. In almost every lab we visited in the satellite countries we found Sergeyev's latest books on brain research being minutely studied. Communist scientists were particularly excited about Sergeyev's new discovery of an unusual aspect of Mikhailova's brain. "Most people generate three or four times more electrical voltage from the back of the brain than the front," said Sergeyev. "Mikhailova's brain generates *fifty times* more voltage from the back of the head than the front." (Of course, even this much electrical discharge in the brain is so faint it has to be amplified four million times just to be recorded and observed.) Sergeyev, who has found this brain pattern in about 7 percent of the people he's ever tested, feels it's a good indicator that they have better than average psychic power.

The second film on Mrs. Mikhailova appeared on the movie screen. "All you've seen so far in the first film is the outer expression of telekinesis. It's PK the way anyone could observe it," Sergeyev said. "Now, with new instruments, we can get some idea of what telekinesis is like from the inside.

We can discover what happens to a human being when PK occurs."

Monitoring Mikhailova's Brain

In this film Mrs. Mikhailova was seated inside the electronically insulated EEG chamber of a Leningrad physiology lab. She was strapped into a leather headpiece that looked like an early aviator's cap, covered with electrodes. Her wrists were braceleted with leather straps and more electrodes. Like an astronaut, she was all trussed up and wired for sound. Instruments measured heartbeat and brain waves. At a distance from her, the new Sergeyev detectors measured the "biological fields" twelve feet away from her body.

As before, Mikhailova began to circle her hands above the objects on the table. Her face creased with strain as she struggled to activate her PK powers. (We've pieced together what happens next from the film, subsequent interviews, and published reports.)

During the revving-up phase, the EEGS showed tremendous activity in the region of the brain controlling sight. Was this explosive activity in this part of her brain one of the reasons she sometimes becomes temporarily blind after a PK test? As she concentrated ferociously, the electrocardiograph showed her heartbeat had increased four times its normal rate, to 240 beats a minute.

The object in front of Mikhailova began to move. Would the new detectors be able to catch PK in action? Suddenly, the Sergeyev detectors revealed something that researchers had never been able to see before. The powerful magnetic fields around Mikhailova's body began to *pulse*! It was as if she'd caused a wave of energy to vibrate through the invisible energy-envelope around her. Brain and heart pulsed in rhythm with these vibrations in her force field! Not only was her entire force field pulsing, the detectors showed that this pulsing force field had *focused* in the direction of her gaze.

But how did this pulsing force field she focused on an object make it move?

"I believe these vibrations in the fields around her body act like magnetic waves," Sergeyev theorized. "The moment these magnetic vibrations or waves occur, they cause the object Mrs. Mikhailova focuses on, even if it's something non-magnetic, to act as if magnetized. It causes the object to be attracted to her or repelled from her."

So "mind over matter" wasn't quite accurate. It was really "mind over force field." This vibrating force field was the mechanism, according to the Soviets, by which the mind could produce at least some kinds of PK. If these tests are right, the Soviets have scored a walloping break-through in PK.

Animals Have ESP

D. Scott Rogo

Many people report instances of ESP involving their pets—for example, when a dog appears to know when its owner will arrive home, even when the owner comes home at different times each day. Scientists too, have found evidence of some animals' predictive ability—for example, animals that seem to be able to predict catastrophic events, such as an earthquake or a tornado. And some dogs are currently being trained as "seizure animals"; they apparently are able to predict when their owner is about to have a seizure, and they take measures to alert and protect that person. But do these instances of unusual animal behavior mean that these animals have a sixth sense, or are they just extrasensitive to the natural cues in their environment? The following article gives an overview of some of the research that has been done to determine if animals have ESP. The author, D. Scott Rogo, was a paranormal investigator who wrote many books and articles on paranormal topics.

Excerpted from "Do Animals Have ESP?" by D. Scott Rogo, *Fate*, July 1986. Copyright © 1986 by Llewellyn Publications. Reprinted with permission.

Stories of pets and other animals with psychic powers have inspired legends and campfire tales. But many of these stories are true. The story of Bobbie, a collie lost by his owners in Indiana, is told in Charles Alexander's *Bobbie: A Great Collie of Oregon* (1926). Bobbie made headlines when he walked for 3,000 miles back home to Silverton, Oregon; it took him six months. The late J.B. Rhine investigated a 1951 case in which a cat, left behind in California, made its way across country to its owners' new home in Oklahoma.

Stories of dogs that howled piteously when their distant masters were killed also abound in literature. Reports of animals predicting disasters have led to studies of the possible psychic abilities of some animals.

For years parapsychologists in this country and in Europe have been experimenting in the laboratory with canine, feline, and rodent subjects. Their work adds a fascinating chapter to the history of parapsychology.

Probably the basic question concerning animal ESP is whether it is widely distributed throughout the animal kingdom. Just how many kinds of animals possess ESP? If ESP is a natural ability, one would expect all animals—not just highly evolved ones like dogs and cats—to possess a sixth sense.

Even Lower Animals Seem to Have a Sixth Sense

This hypothesis has led some researchers to experiment with primitive animal forms, to see if they have some extrasensory powers. Parapsychologists in Great Britain, for example, demonstrated back in the 1950s and 1960s that even the tiny paramecia (one-celled animals visible only through a microscope) and wood lice can at least receive ESP messages. The experimenters placed the little critters on glass plates and then "willed" them to swim or crawl up, down, left or right. A different direction was chosen for each trial, of course. This simple experiment was repeated over and over and the animals often moved in the direction toward which they were telepathically commanded. Similar experiments have been conducted with sea worms, caterpillars, and ants.

Even fish seem to possess ESP powers. Dr. Robert Morris, a former colleague of mine at the Psychical Research Foundation in Durham, North Carolina, demonstrated this when he was still working at the Institute for Parapsychology (also located in Durham). . . .

Morris used a simple T-maze for his experiment. An animal is released at the base of the "T" and will be forced to turn either left or right when it reaches the junction at the cross-area of the stem. Morris filled the T-maze with water, released fish into it and tried to will them to turn either to the left or to the right. His attempts were only marginally significant.

Morris designed a more complicated experiment to test the fish for precognition. This test also was conducted under the auspices of the Institute for Parapsychology. Morris, an animal behaviorist, knew that fish become agitated when facing a threatening situation, so he placed three goldfish in a tank and had an assistant monitor their behavior to determine which fish acted most agitated—which fish swam about most.

After the assistant had made his observations, Morris caught one of the fish in a net and held it aloft over the tank—which should be a highly traumatic experience for a fish! He chose the fish randomly, but found that often the one he caught in his little net was the fish his assistant had designated the most "agitated." He concluded that the fish had actually foreseen this life-threatening experience.

The results of this experiment, however, were still only marginal. Morris decided that the results were not stable, reliable, or replicable.

Mouse ESP?

Very little work was done with animals during the 1950s and '60s. Most parapsychologists felt it was more fruitful to work with people than with fish, dogs, cats, or rodents. The research done with animals was intriguing but did not show strong results. All this was soon to change. The world of animal ESP research (anpsi research, for short) received a boost in 1968 when two French scientists, writing under the pseudonyms of Pierre Duval and Evelyn Montredon, reported their new technique for testing the ESP powers of mice. This experiment was easy to run, harmless to the animals, and, according to the scientists, highly reliable. They conducted their research at the Sorbonne in Paris.

The design of the Duval-Montredon experiment was simple. The scientists used a specially constructed box which was divided in half by a low barrier. A grid capable of conducting an electrical current was placed at the bottom of the cage. The box was then hooked up to a generator which delivered a series of shocks to either side of the cage in random order. A shock was sent every minute or so. Since most animals have a strong aversion to electrical shock, the experimenters wished to determine whether mice placed in the apparatus could determine precognitively which side of the box was about to receive the shock and so jump over the barrier and escape it.

The mice did, of course, jump over the barrier when they received a shock; this was a normal response to the discomfort. But the French researchers noted especially those moments when the mice jumped across the barrier for no apparent reason. These they called "random behavior trials." By testing the mice over and over again, they discovered that the rodents tended to jump over the barrier when the side of the cage in which they had been placed was about to be shocked. This tendency was too consistent to have been the result of coincidence. The mice seemed to know when and where the shock was coming, and jumped the barrier to avoid it.

Duval and Montredon conducted a series of these tests before submitting their research to the *Journal of Parapsychology*, the official publication of the Institute of Parapsychology. The Durham people were excited when they learned of these experiments because it seemed the French researchers had discovered a consistent way of studying ESP in animals.

The task of replicating the French rodent research fell to W.J. Levy, a young doctor who had only recently joined the Institute staff. Dr. Levy reported a series of consistent replications of the French research. In 1974, however, this research was called into question when he was caught faking some of his later research, so it is an open question whether the French work was really confirmed at Rhine's laboratory.

Humane Experiments

Although fascinated by the original Duval-Montredon work and Levy's alleged replication of it, European researchers were unhappy that the animals were punished by shocks if they didn't show psychic capabilities. Consequently, several of them began designing rodent-ESP tests which rewarded rather than punished the animals if they succeeded. This allowed them to conduct their tests with a clearer conscience.

Some of the first work along these lines was done by Sybo Schouten at the University of Utrecht, which has long maintained an excellent parapsychology laboratory. Schouten planned to see if his mice could use ESP to get nourishment. He began by training the mice in a special cage equipped with a water-feeding tube. A lever inside the cage controlled the feeding system. A light bulb, also located inside, was the key to success. The mice were taught that they could get a drop of water by pulling the lever down, but only when the light bulb flashed on.

After the mice had learned how to work the lever and water system, they were tested for ESP. They were placed in a new box which had two levers. A generator randomly determined that only one of the levers would release water from the tube at any given time. Schouten hoped that each mouse being tested would be able to choose the correct lever, once the light bulb went on. The test was successful since, after a great many trials, Schouten was able to determine that the mice were choosing the correct lever more than the expected fifty percent of the time.

Schouten went on to design what may be called the first experiment in "mouse telepathy." He conducted the same experiment outlined above but with one catch. A second mouse was placed in a separate, but identical box, and was shown which was the correct lever to push. It was Schouten's idea that the second mouse might be able telepathically to inform his little cousin which lever to choose. This experiment was also successful.

Researchers in England also began to test rodents for ESP by using rewards instead of punishments. They too were successful.

Another intriguing development came to parapsychology's attention during this time. The fuss and furor caused by the Duval-Montredon work gradually led some parapsychologists to ask an even more provocative question. If animals can make psychic contact with the outside world through some sort of sixth sense, might they also be capable of controlling it? In other words, do animals possess psychokinesis as well as ESP?

Cockroaches with PK?

The pioneering work in this controversial area of parapsychology was the brainchild of Helmut Schmidt, a German physicist who first settled in Seattle where he worked with the Boeing Laboratories. Because of his interest in parapsychology, he eventually moved to Durham, where he joined the staff of the Institute for Parapsychology. His first experiments were with very simple forms of life, such as algae, and even yeast cultures. Not until he began working with cockroaches did he hit the jackpot.

Dr. Schmidt conducted his first successful experiment at the Institute in 1970. He placed cockroaches on an electric grid which was hooked to a generator. At regular intervals the generator would activate and either deliver a shock to the grid or withhold it. Shock delivery was entirely random. This meant that when the cockroaches were placed on the grid for a series of trials, the generator would deliver shocks only fifty percent of the times it was activated. Schmidt believed that, if the cockroaches possessed PK ability, they would use their powers to zap the inner workings of the generator and cause it to malfunction so that it would deliver shocks somewhat less than fifty percent of the time.

Schmidt tested several cockroaches before making an amazing discovery. It seemed the cockroaches were causing the generator to deliver more shocks than expected. Apparently the insects were seeking out the shocks as a form of stimulation!

The finding alerted Schmidt to a major problem in all parapsychology research. Since he had run the tests with the cockroaches himself, he might have used his own PK on the generator. Schmidt acknowledged that he didn't like working with cockroaches, so his own aversion might have led him unconsciously to punish the insects by zapping the generator into producing more shocks than it should have.

A Cat Turns Up the Heat

For his next test, Schmidt used his pet cat, and automated the experiment so that he wouldn't have to monitor it. He placed the cat in a shed behind his home in Durham. It gets pretty cold there at night and the only source of heat in the shed was an electric lamp hooked to a generator which randomly turned it on and off. The lamp was programmed to stay on precisely fifty percent of the time in order to stay warm. Since the test was automated, Schmidt left the shed for the duration of the experiment. By remaining inside his house when the test was being run, the physicist hoped that no PK would escape from his mind to help his pet.

The test results confirmed Schmidt's hypothesis. The cat was able to make the light stay on more than fifty percent of the time. Schmidt never was able to replicate this experiment, however. The temperature in Durham started to warm up, and the cat soon learned to hate the shed. She would run away as soon as anyone tried to get her inside.

Schmidt's PK test with the heat lamp prompted other researchers at the Institute for Parapsychology to design similar experiments. They attempted replication using lizards, chicks, and even unhatched chicken embryos, and reported some success. Although there has been relatively little research conducted to explore the PK powers of animals, most of the work that has been done has followed closely along the lines of Schmidt's original experiment. The only major exception was a clever experiment run by William Braud of the Mind Science Foundation in San Antonio, Texas.

Something Fishy

Dr. Braud, a soft-spoken young psychologist, spent most of his early career studying the learning capacities of freshwater fish at the University of Houston, before turning to parapsychology. His interest in parapsychology led him to join the staff of the Mind Science Foundation, where he decided to test the possibility that fish possess PK.

He designed a novel test to explore this possibility. First he procured two Siamese fighting fish. These fish are so aggressive that they will attack their own reflections. They were placed in a special tank equipped with a mirror which could be turned either toward or away from the fish. The mirror was then hooked to a generator which produced a high-speed oscillation. As long as the generator was running smoothly, it turned the mirror toward the tank a specific number of times. As soon as the fish saw their reflections, they would become agitated; they would change color, extend their gills, beat their tails and put on quite a show.

Braud theorized that the naturally aggressive fish would use PK to interfere with the oscillations produced by the generator, and cause the mirror to turn toward them more frequently than it would under normal circumstances.

He was right. After several days of testing, Braud discovered that the fighting fish did seem capable of affecting the mirror oscillations. To check his finding, he also tested two other species of aggressive fish, as well as common goldfish, which are rather placid. As he expected, the aggressive fish all affected the generator, while the goldfish did not.

Animal PK, unfortunately, has not been as thoroughly researched as has animal ESP. Consequently it is hard to draw any firm conclusions from the relatively few studies conducted to date. Do these studies really indicate that animals possess psychokinetic abilities? It is practically impossible to tell whether the animals are employing their PK powers, or whether the experimenter is contributing the talent himself.

Clairvoyant Dogs?

Although many cases of telepathic dogs have come to parapsychology's attention over the years, there has been relatively little experimental exploration to determine whether dogs generally are psychic. Among the work that has been done were some U.S. Army–sponsored experiments conducted by J.B. Rhine while he was still at Duke University.

In 1952, representatives of the army asked Dr. Rhine if he thought dogs could be trained to locate mines buried in battlefields. This was a serious concern of the military. If dogs did possess such a clairvoyant capability, many lives could be saved. Rhine said he would be willing to experiment and try to find out. The army supplied the funds for the project; its only condition was that the tests must be kept secret.

The tests were conducted in California, along a beach north of San Francisco. Rhine's colleagues buried five small wooden boxes to serve as "dummy" mines along the shoreline for each test. Then a dog trainer, who did not know where the boxes were buried, would lead his dogs along the beach and mark the spots where the dogs indicated a mine was buried. The dogs were trained to sit down when they detected one of the boxes.

Over a three-month period, 203 tests were run. The dogs successfully located the mines a little more than fifty percent of the time. This is above what coincidence could account for; the dogs, however, tended to do best at the beginning of the test and then their accuracy diminished.

The U.S. Army eventually abandoned the test because the results weren't consistent enough and training dogs' ESP seemed impractical. The army's main concern was that the dogs seemed incapable of independently searching out and locating the mines; they had to be led through the mock minefield by a trainer.

Canine Psychics

Probably the most sophisticated experimental work with canine subjects was conducted by Aristed Esser, a psychiatrist at Rockland State Hospital in New York. In 1975 he undertook a series of ingenious tests, apparently prompted by rumors that Soviet scientists were testing animals for ESP. One of these rumors alleged that Soviet officials had sent out a submarine carrying baby rabbits, while the mother rabbit was kept at a laboratory on the mainland. The story was that when the baby rabbits were either killed or frightened, the mother became agitated at that very same moment. The truth or falsity of this story has never been determined. Nonetheless, the report gave Dr. Esser the idea for his tests.

Esser's tests were to determine whether dogs could respond telepathically when their masters or canine cousins were threatened in any way. In one initial experiment, he made use of two rooms located at different ends of the hospital in which he worked. Two beagles, trained as hunting dogs, were placed in one of the rooms. This room had an observation window which led to an adjoining area, so the dogs could be watched carefully during the test. The owner of the dogs was escorted to the other chamber, given an airgun and instructed to "shoot" at colored slides of animals flashed on a wall of the room at random intervals. The experimenters then waited to see how the dogs would react during the "shootings." The dogs barked and whined as soon as the hunter started shooting, even though they could neither see nor hear what was going on in the chamber where he was positioned.

Esser was so pleased with his results that when he reported his experiments in 1967 he said he had "no doubt . . . that some dogs, especially those with a close relationship with their owner, have highly developed ESP."

A Dog with Heart

Esser conducted a series of follow-up tests. One of these was designed to see if a boxer would react when its owner was threatened. The dog was placed in a soundproof room and attached to a device that kept a record of its heartbeat. The dog's owner, a young woman who had volunteered to take part in the experiment, was asked to wait in a different room in another part of the hospital. She had no idea that the experiment had already begun, so she was startled when a mysterious man barged into the room and shouted wildly. Of course this was all part of the plan. At the exact time the woman was so badly frightened, her dog's heartbeat suddenly accelerated for no apparent reason. The boxer apparently sensed that its owner was in trouble and became agitated.

The doctor conducted a similar test using two boxers. One was a female, the other her male offspring. Each dog was placed in a separate room. When one of the experimenters threatened the younger dog with a newspaper, the mother dog was seen suddenly to cower in the other room.

I think the experiments we have discussed have been fruitful. Other parapsychologists have their own view about the importance and success of animal ESP research.

Dr. Morris, probably the world's leading authority on animal ESP, has acknowledged that "there is some evidence that psi communication is not restricted to humans," but he refuses to speculate on the meaning of his work. "Before more specific speculation on the evolution of psi and its ecological significance can be seriously considered," he wrote in 1977, "we need more data on more species." He points out that, while it certainly appears animals possess ESP, we still know virtually nothing about the hows, whys, and wherefores of their capacities. We are especially in the dark about the conditions under which animals can be expected to make use of their psychic powers.

John Randall, a biologist who pioneered research on ESP in animals in Great Britain, is much more enthusiastic about the evidence. Nor does he hesitate to speculate about the long-range meaning of this work. He believes ESP may have been a power which significantly guided and shaped the process of evolution itself.

Parapsychologists are not the only scientists intrigued by the new vistas opened up by the discovery of ESP in animals. Many conventional zoologists are excited by the evidence. They speculate that ESP may be an "X" factor which contributes to the hive behavior of communal insects such as ants and bees, helps pigeons home, controls the behavior of migrating birds and assists animals in adapting to their environments.

These ideas are speculative, but they remain scientific possibilities. Only time will tell what role ESP plays in the daily lives of animals, but the evidence that they do possess ESP seems unimpeachable.

A Reporter's Ganzfeld Experience

Mary Roach

Of all of the controlled scientific research about ESP, experiments called ganzfeld ("uniform field") have shown the most possibility of providing incontrovertible proof that ESP exists. Ganzfeld experiments involve two participants: a sender and a receiver, also called a viewer. The receiver is placed in an environment in which sensory stimulation is prevented as much as possible. For example, the receiver's eyes may be covered, and the room may be dark and soundproof except for a kind of background noise called white noise, which covers up distracting sounds. The sender, in another location, tries to telepathically send an image to the receiver—that is, by mind power alone. During the 1990s several series of Ganzfeld experiments yielded positive results. The author of this article, Mary Roach, is a magazine reporter who wanted to find out more about how Ganzfeld experiments work—and participate in an experiment herself. She met with psychologist and

Ganzfeld researcher Robert Morris, a psychology professor at the University of Edinburgh. This is Roach's account of her Ganzfeld experience.

Telepathy is defined as extrasensory communication between two minds. Yours and mine, for example. According to ongoing research, we might, under certain circumstances, actually be able to sense one another's thoughts. As it happens, I have a pretty good idea about yours right now. You are thinking, This woman is an idiot. She's a New Age dingdong, and I can't believe they're doing this story.

I confess I didn't use telepathy to figure this out. I used empathy. I thought the same thing when I saw an article in Britain's *New Scientist.* "Psychic research has long been written off as the stuff of cranks and frauds," read the teaser. "But there's now one telepathy experiment that leaves even the skeptics scratching their heads."

The experiment in question involves a set-up called the *ganzfeld.* A subject sits in a soundproof room, while down the hall a "sender" watches a repeating video clip and attempts to mentally transmit the image on the screen. Afterward, the subject is shown four images and asked which one was "sent." Bare chance would dictate a correct choice one in four times. So far, the average hit rate has been closer to one in three. It doesn't sound like much of a difference, but statistically this is hot stuff. The odds that a success rate of roughly 33 percent could be due to a run of good guesses are less than one in a million.

Something Unexplained

The statistics don't necessarily mean that everyone has telepathic abilities. They *do* suggest that something unexplained is taking place—that some people, sometimes, may be able to communicate when the laws of physics say it's impossible.

In January 1994, a paper on a series of ganzfeld experiments appeared in *Psychological Bulletin*. It was the first telepathy research in nearly 25 years to pass muster at a major peer-reviewed psychology journal. What set these and a few earlier ganzfeld studies apart is that they represent a unique collaboration: that of a group of parapsychologists and a noted skeptic, Ray Hyman, of the Committee for the Scientific Investigation (read: the Debunking and General Ridicule) of Claims of the Paranormal.

The equipment and procedures have been devised and repeatedly modified to address Hyman's criticisms; parapsychologists have made their own improvements, too. For example, to prevent researcher fraud or tampering by hackers, a computer now prints hard copies of each subject's data. The printouts go to three experimenters, none of whom knows where the other copies are kept. To preclude any high-tech cheating between sender and receiver, subjects are paired with strangers (a painful concession, as experiments pairing friends typically yield a better outcome).

When an analysis of assorted ganzfeld studies revealed the one-in-three hit rate, Hyman ate his hat: "If independent laboratories can produce similar results . . . with the same attention to rigorous methodology," he wrote, "then parapsychology may indeed have finally captured its elusive quarry."

Replication Efforts

Attempts at replication are underway at four ganzfeld chambers worldwide. The busiest and best known is run by Robert Morris, a psychologist at the University of Edinburgh, in Scotland. Morris himself is not Scottish. He comes from Pennsylvania. Soft-spoken, deferential, myopic, he is as unmystical a man as you are likely to meet. He plays bad-

minton and drives an aging Datsun. Under his desk is a pair
of bedroom slippers that he wears when he works late,
which he almost always does. At the moment he is sitting
with one leg tucked beneath him, sipping nettle tea.

Morris has handed me a lengthy ganzfeld paper, many
busy pages of chi squares and Stanford z scores. I skip ahead
to the heading "Examples of Target-Mentation Correspon-
dences." This is parapsychology speak for 16 Really Amazing Examples of What Looks to Be Telepathy in Action. Here
is one of them:

Series: 301, Participant ID: 146

*Target 22, Spiders: A spider is weaving its web. The spider's long
legs spring up and down repeatedly, weaving strands of the web.*

Subject Mentation (that is, the receiver's stream-of-
consciousness chatter): *"The veins of a windmill . . . something
like a spider web . . . like basket weaving. . . . An image of . . . a
pogo stick . . . something in which you jumped up and down. . . ."*

"Bear in mind," cautions Morris, "those 16 passages were
selected from over 350 sessions—the Top of the Pops, if you
will." He further points out that the mentations were edited
down to illustrate the correspondence; the passages are isolated sentences and fragments taken from what sometimes
amounts to six or seven pages of transcription.

I ask Morris if I can take a turn in the ganzfeld, and he
tells me to come back Saturday morning. Not that I'm ex-
pecting anything dramatic. To date, my psychic experience
amounts to sixth-grade Ouija board sessions. (I moved it.)

A Ganzfeld Experience

Edinburgh in spring is a monochrome of slate and slush.
There are goose pimples on the knees of the Royal Mile bag-
pipers and salt stains on the patent leather boots of the
Scotch Royal Guard. In two days of wandering the city, I've
become a connoisseur of warm places to sit. The Portrait

Gallery is nice, as is the Scotsmans Lounge, but top rank goes to the sound-isolation room at the University of Edinburgh, a.k.a. the ganzfeld chamber. You are seated in a recliner and given a blanket for your feet. They pour tea and serve you McVitties digestive biscuits.

The advantage of the Portrait Gallery is that no one comes along and tapes Ping-Pong balls over your eyes. More precisely, they are Ping-Pong ball halves, cut and sanded by graduate student Kathy Dalton. Anyone familiar with The Who's *Tommy* knows just exactly how foolish I look right now. Dalton hands me headphones, which will be playing white noise. Morris explains the setup. If some sort of very weak extrasensory signal is coming through, it's more likely to be detected with no interference from the outside world. (*Ganzfeld* means "uniform field"—an empty vista for the eyes, static for the ears.) Sensory deprivation is lazy man's meditation; with nothing to see or hear, the mind shifts its focus inward.

Morris will be my sender. Being someone's sender is not unlike being someone's Valentine. You sit alone in a room, thinking of one person and one thought, and hoping that person is thinking the same thing. Morris will be watching the video image and attempting to telepathically transmit it through the four-inch Sonex Acoustical Padding, down the hall, and into my head. Morris describes his technique as "trying to get very absorbed in the image, experiencing it as fully as I can," while acting as a sort of "beacon" guiding the subject's thoughts.

He clips a microphone to my shirt, which will feed into his and Dalton's headsets. Dalton will be next door taking notes on my mentation. I've been told to speak out loud any images and thoughts that pass through my mind over the course of the next half hour.

So far, there's not a lot worth sharing.

Series: 01. Participant ID: 43

Subject Mentation: "*Gosh, those McVitties really stick in your teeth. My foot itches. Is the Scotch Whisky Heritage Centre open on Sundays?*"

I am, in fact, a lousy candidate. Those who perform well in the ganzfeld tend to share certain traits, all of which I lack. Most report having had some sort of paranormal experience in the past. Many have had practice with internal attention states such as meditation or hypnosis. The attribute most strongly linked to telepathic prowess is musical or artistic creativity. One of the highest success rates to date comes from a study of students at The Juilliard School, half of whom correctly picked the image that was being sent—nearly double the rate among the general population.

Toward the end of the half hour, a few faint images come and go: a forest, a Tudor building, a lizard, the Ice Capades, a hand.

Experiment Over

The half hour up, Dalton cues my four video choices on the TV to my left. A flying dove, a collapsing bridge, a scene from *Star Wars*. Nothing looks familiar. The last clip is from *Becket:* Richard Burton is being consecrated Archbishop of Canterbury. Unless ice dancers or reptiles descend on the abbey, it looks like a bust. The film cuts to a close-up of the bishop's gloved hand. A hand! I choose clip four.

The fourth clip is in fact the one Morris had been "sending." He shows me a paper covered with doodles. (Drawing parts of the image helps him concentrate.) On it is an outline of a disembodied hand, which Morris says he'd just drawn when I mentioned seeing a hand.

Back in Morris's office, I prattle excitedly about my new-found possibly-but-who-knows abilities. Morris nods politely. He's circumspect about any individual ganzfeld session, the results of which could be due to chance; it's the series as a whole, he says, that has him "90 percent persuaded there's really something quite new going on here."

As for just what that something might be—folds in the space-time continuum? extra-strong brain waves?—Morris hasn't a clue. "That hasn't been our focus. We're trying to come at it from the bottom up, not the top down. We are simply saying, 'People have unusual experiences; we would like to learn as much about them as possible.'"

But what does he think—was my experience telepathy or coincidence? Morris smiles. He is looking at my empty teacup "I think," he says sagely, "that you should have some more tea."

The CIA Successfully Used Psychic Spies

James Schnabel

For twenty-two years, from 1972 to 1994, the U.S. Central Intelligence Agency (CIA) and other government agencies were involved in efforts to discover if ESP could be used as a spy tool. The government's interest was sparked by news leaked or smuggled out of the secretive Soviet Union that the USSR was doing advanced research with ESP and in fact might be using ESP to spy on the United States and other Western countries. There was fear that the Soviet Union was even able to affect Western military efforts through mental power.

In the following article the author describes two incidents involving one of the U.S. program's most successful "psychic spies," Joe McMoneagle. McMoneagle was "a bull-necked [army] warrant officer" who had had a near-death experience (he was "dead" for a short period of time) that apparently awakened his remote viewing abilities. The program's operating officer at the time the following events took place was Lieutenant Skip Atwater. Project Grill Flame is what the program was known as during this time. (It had several names over its history and is perhaps best known by its final name, Star Gate.)

Jim Schnabel is a science writer and the author of three books about paranormal topics.

Among other things, McMoneagle's Celtic genes and Austrian near-death experience seemed to have given him a very useful ability—the ability to remain semialert while descending into a dreamlike state of consciousness. Most people achieved such a state, sometimes called "vivid dreaming," only once in a while, perhaps after a too-heavy meal, or during an illness. But McMoneagle seemed able to enter this magical zone almost at will.

As a result, his remote-viewing visions had a remarkable realism and narrative consistency. After a session down in his zone, he could often recall and sketch what he had seen down to the tiniest detail. Even during the session, he was occasionally able to describe scenes just as if he were watching a film in a theater. It could be that easy.

At times, however, certain strange perceptual distortions crept in that required subtle interpretation. One day in about 1980, a client in the intelligence community came to the Fort Meade unit with a special tasking. The client wanted the remote viewers to track the movements of a person, apparently a foreign agent based in Europe, at certain specific times—every twelve hours or so—over a period of several days in the recent past.

Atwater soon ran McMoneagle against the target. The target folder had the agent's photograph inside. On the outside were the specified dates and times when the client wanted to know what he had been doing. Atwater told McMoneagle the target was a person; his task was to describe the person and his surroundings at the times written on the envelope.

McMoneagle sank down into his zone, and began to run through the list of times. For one of the specified times, he sensed a road. It wound through hills. He realized that the target was the driver of a car on this road. He was male, dark-haired, neatly dressed, perhaps a businessman. Mc-Moneagle described the road, and the hills, and the car, and then about five minutes into the session, something about the target changed. McMoneagle became confused. "The guy's going somewhere I can't go," he said. "What do you mean?" asked Atwater. "Well," said McMoneagle, "it's like I was looking at his picture and the picture turned sideways." The target had suddenly vanished.

Later, after delivering the session results to the client, Atwater learned that the man in the photograph had failed to appear for a meeting with his case officer. That was why the client had wanted to retrospectively track his movements. Some time after the remote viewers turned in their data, the client discovered that the man—at the point in time where Joe McMoneagle had remote-viewed him—had somehow lost control of his car on a winding road in Italy, and had plunged over a cliff to his death.

Gone Fishing?

At CIA headquarters one day, Norm Everheart was telephoned by a man he knew from the FBI. The FBI man, who knew about Grill Flame, had a counterintelligence situation that he hoped the remote viewers could help him with. There was one hitch, however. The FBI man was unable to task the remote viewers himself. His boss, on religious or skeptical grounds, or both, refused to let him have any dealings at all with Grill Flame's psychics. Therefore the FBI man had come to Norm Everheart. Could Everheart handle this for him, under the table? Everheart, a relatively friendly, easygoing man in what was generally a cold and conniving business, said he would be happy to help.

The situation the FBI man was concerned about had come to his attention through sheer luck. On a recent morning, at about six, a local police officer somewhere in suburban Maryland had stopped a car that had gone too quickly past a stop sign. The police officer saw that the car had diplomatic plates. He walked up to the driver's-side window, and asked to see the driver's license and registration. The driver, as was clear from the documents, was a senior Soviet Embassy official. He was dressed in a business suit, and he was clearly annoyed at having been stopped. Across the backseat of his car, the officer noted, the embassy man had a fishing pole. The policeman's report soon landed at the FBI's Soviet counterintelligence office.

A fishing pole . . . What would a Soviet intelligence officer—assuming that that was what he was—have been doing dressed in a business suit at 6:00 A.M., driving in suburban Maryland with a fishing pole in his backseat?

Norm Everheart found it odd, too. And it wasn't the first such case he had heard of. Fishing poles seemed to be sprouting up all over the Soviet diplomatic corps. Either the Soviets were becoming avid fishermen, or the fishing poles concealed some kind of electronic gadget—perhaps a covert communications device or a SIGINT [Signals Intelligence, a military intelligence program] collection system.

Everheart knew of a recent case, in some other country, where the host intelligence service had noticed that a certain Soviet Embassy employee always went out to a certain lake to fish, while some local official—perhaps his agent—fished on the opposite side. Were they communicating hydrophonically, through the poles? An operation was mounted to find out, but nothing ever came of it.

Whatever was going on, the Soviets who possessed the poles seemed to regard them as incredibly sensitive and valuable. One day, somewhere in Scandinavia, a Soviet Embassy man had been involved in a serious auto accident. He had been lying in his car, bleeding and badly injured, as the paramedics worked on him, but he had loudly refused to be taken to the hospital. He had insisted upon waiting until his colleagues at the embassy arrived and took from him the things he clutched tightly in his hand—five of the mysterious fishing poles.

In some cases, the Soviets took pains to create the impression that they really did like to fish with those ubiquitous poles. In a certain capital city in Africa, a group of Soviet Embassy officials—paired as husbands and wives—had developed the habit of going out to a lake in a boat, and sitting there with their fishing poles for hours, apparently fishing. CIA eavesdropping specialists had eventually managed to plant a listening device in the boat, through which they heard the wives complaining: *It was Olga's turn to go this week. Why do I have to be here?* And so forth. None of the Soviets said anything that was particularly incriminating, but they clearly regarded this as a duty, rather than recreation. Everheart hoped that the remote viewers would clear up the mystery once and for all.

Seeking the Target

Joe McMoneagle was one of the first to go after the target. All he knew was that the target was a person whose picture was in the target envelope, at some unstated location at some unstated time. He sank down into his zone and saw a man driving his car, and being stopped by a policeman. The man was dressed in a business suit. He spoke Russian. He had a fishing pole in his backseat. Atwater didn't even know the fishing pole was supposed to be there; Norm Everheart, with his usual oblique targeting method, hadn't told him. But now Atwater realized the pole was important, and he directed McMoneagle to press the attack. What was the significance of the fishing pole? How did the man in the car intend to use it?

McMoneagle decided to ask the man in the car. *What are you going to do with that fishing pole?* This was an especially strange use of the telepathic interrogation technique, since the target was not only at a different place, but at a different *time*, at least several days in the past.

Whatever was really happening, McMoneagle seemed to interrogate the KGB man for a while, and then he followed his journey in the car with the pole: The KGB man drove to a wooded area at the edge of a sensitive military installation, which was surrounded by a high perimeter fence. At one point the fence was interrupted by a tall building, and about fifteen feet up the outer wall of the building there was a loose piece of masonry. The KGB man walked up to the building and telescoped out his fishing pole. He used it to reach up and dislodge a small package that some Soviet-controlled American agent, presumably working at the installation, had wedged into the wall by the loose masonry.

When Everheart read the remote viewer's data, his heart sank. It just didn't seem right. In all the other cases in which the pole had made its appearance, it had seemed to harbor some kind of sophisticated electronic device. But according to the remote viewer, the pole was simply being used as a mechanical aid, to service what spies called a "dead-drop" site, a secret place where agents stashed film or other materials for collection by their case officers. Even so, Everheart passed the information on to the man at the FBI. Later he heard that the FBI had staked out the site by the military installation, and had seen the KGB officer using the pole to dislodge something from a chink high up in the side of the building.

McMoneagle had not only been incredibly accurate—he had helped to break an important case. Now Norm Everheart began to wonder about all the other fishing pole stories. Were the Soviets using the poles simply to hide and retrieve material at elevated and otherwise inaccessible dead-drops? Everheart never knew, but he was satisfied that he had found the answer in at least this one episode.

Laboratory Studies Suggest That ESP Is Real

Dean Radin

Scientists have formally studied ESP in laboratories since the beginning of the twentieth century. Many scientific studies have shown encouraging results, but mainstream science generally shows little interest, and skeptics consistently find flaws in the way the studies are designed or carried out. Nevertheless, a few scientists, including this article's author, Dean Radin, believe that real progress is being made. Radin has studied ESP and related phenomenon for many years, working, teaching, and conducting studies for private corporations and at universities. He is president of the Boundary Institute, a parapsychological research organization. He is the author of *The Conscious Universe*, which provides a good overview of research involving ESP.

Alex, a university colleague, was cleaning his double-action, six-shot revolver in preparation for a haunting trip later in the month. In this pistol, when the trigger is pulled the hammer is cocked, the cylinder revolves, and the hammer falls on the next chamber, all in one smooth motion. For safety's sake, Alex normally kept five bullets in the revolver, with the hammer resting on the sixth, empty chamber.

Before cleaning the gun, he later told me, he removed the five bullets and set them aside. When finished cleaning, he begun to put the bullets back in the cylinder. When he arrived at the fifth and final bullet, he suddenly got a distinct sense of dread. It had something to do with that bullet.

Alex was bothered about the odd feeling because nothing like it had ever happened to him before. He decided to trust his gut, so he put the bullet aside and positioned the pistol's hammer as usual over the sixth chamber. The chamber next to it, which normally held the fifth bullet, was now also empty.

Two weeks later, Alex was at a hunting lodge with his fiancée and her parents. That evening, unexpectedly, a violent argument broke out between the parents. Alex tried to calm them down, but the father, in an insane rage, grabbed Alex's gun, which had been in a drawer, and pointed it at his wife.

Alex tried to intervene by jumping between the gun and the woman, but he was too late—the trigger was already being pulled. For a horrifying split second, Alex knew that he was about to get shot at point-blank range. But instead of a sudden, gruesome death, the pistol went "click." The cylinder had revolved to an empty chamber—the very chamber that would have contained the fifth bullet if Alex had not set it aside two weeks earlier.

Had Alex actually predicted the future, or was this just an extraordinary coincidence? There are several possible explanations for why such "intuitive hunches" sometimes play out. One is that on a subconscious level, we are always thinking and coming to conclusions, but that these register only as hunches to our conscious mind. Another is that we pick up telling cues from body language, subliminal sounds or peripheral vision without being consciously aware of doing so. A third is that for each amazing coincidence we remember, we forget all the times we had a hunch and it didn't pan out. A fourth possibility is that we modify our memories for our own convenience, creating a connection where it may not have existed. And so on. These sorts of prosaic explanations probably account for many intuitive hunches. But they don't explain them all.

As in the case of Alex's intuition, a series of carefully documented case studies raises the possibility that some intuitions are due to a genuine sixth sense. But to confirm that those stories are what they appear to be, we must turn to controlled laboratory tests.

In a pilot study and in three follow-up experiments, I have observed that many people respond unconsciously to something bad—even before it happens. Take the prototypical case of a well-known editor of a popular magazine. When she asks the question, "Is there a sixth sense?" I don't answer directly. I ask if she'd like to participate in an experiment that uses pictures randomly selected by computer and she agrees.

I have her sit before a blank computer screen. All I've told her is that she's about to see a series of digitized photographs. Some will be calm, like a placid lake, and others will be emotional, like a big spider. On two fingers of her left hand, I attach electrodes that measure tiny changes in her skin resistance. On a third finger I place an electrode that monitors blood flow. I explain that all she has to do is press the button on the mouse when she's ready to begin, and then look at the pictures.

I leave the room, she relaxes, and then she presses the button. For five seconds, the screen remains blank, and then the computer randomly selects one picture out of a large pool of photos—some calming and some provocative. The picture is displayed for three seconds, and then the screen goes blank for eight seconds. Finally, a message appears announcing that she can start the next trial whenever she's ready.

She repeats this sequence 40 times. At the end of the experiment, I analyze the data recorded by the electrodes and prepare two summary graphs. Each graph shows average changes in her skin resistance and blood flow before, during and after she saw either calm or emotional pictures. What she immediately notices is that after she viewed the emotional pictures, both her skin resistance and fingertip blood flow dramatically changed. And after she viewed calm pictures, her physiology hardly changed at all.

"So I responded emotionally when I saw something emotional, and I remained calm when I saw something calm," she says. "How does that demonstrate a sixth sense?"

I direct her attention to the segment of the graph showing her responses before the computer selected the pictures. "This bump shows that your body responded to emotional pictures before the computer selected them. And this flat line," I say, pointing to the other line, "shows that your body did not respond before calm pictures were shown. You see? Your body was responding to your future emotion before the computer randomly selected an emotional or calm picture."

Laboratory Proof

As this sinks in, I add, "We can now demonstrate in the laboratory what at some level we've known all along: Many people literally get a gut feeling before something bad happens. Our viscera warn us of danger even if our conscious mind doesn't always get the message."

Our editor's body showed signs of what I call presentiment, an unconscious form of "psi" perception. Psi is a neutral term for psychic experiences, and though it sounds like fodder for an episode of the "X-Files," scientists around the world have studied the subject in the laboratory for over a century. The scientific evidence is now stronger than ever for commonly reported experiences such as telepathy (mind-to-mind communication), clairvoyance (information received from a distant place) and precognition (information received from a distant time). Studies suggest that we have ways of gaining information that bypass the ordinary senses. The sixth sense and similar terms, like second sight and extrasensory perception (ESP), refer to perceptual experiences that transcend the usual boundaries of space and time.

In trying to take these findings further, I realized that we have to dig deeper than what's detectable at the conscious level. While ESP and psi generally refer to conscious psychic experiences, I've always thought that asking people to consciously report subtle psi impressions was a shot in the dark. What would happen if we bypassed the psychological defense mechanisms that filter our perceptions and censor our conscious awareness? Would we find psi experiences that people weren't aware of?

A handful of colleagues have paved the way for this type of investigation. In the mid-1960s, psychologist Charles Tart, Ph.D., of the University of California at Davis, measured skin conductance, blood volume, heart rate, and verbal reports between two people, called a sender-receiver pair. He, as the sender, received random electrical shocks to see if remote receivers could detect those events. Tart found that while they weren't consciously aware of anything out of the ordinary, the distant receivers' physiology registered significant reactions to the shocks he experienced.

In other, independent experiments, engineer Douglas

Dean at the Newark College of Engineering; psychologist Jean Barry, Ph.D., in France; and psychologist Erlendur Haraldsson, Ph.D., at the University of Utrecht [in The Netherlands], all observed significant changes in receivers' finger blood volume when a sender, located thousands of miles away, directed emotional thoughts toward them. The journal *Science* also published a study by two physiologists who reported finding significant correlations in brain waves between isolated identical twins. These sorts of studies came to be known as Distant Mental Intention on Living Systems (DMILS).

Studying Intuitive Hunches

The idea for studying intuitive hunches came to me in 1993, while I was a research fellow in the psychology department at the University of Edinburgh in Scotland. I was investigating the "feeling of being stared at." In the laboratory, I separated two people, placing them in rooms that were 100 feet away from each another. Then I monitored person #1's electrodermal activity while person #2 stared at person #1 over a one-way closed-circuit video system. Although the stared-at person could have no conscious idea when the "starer" was doing the looking, since the two were in different rooms and the staring occurred at random times, I did observe small changes in the skin resistance of the person being stared at over closed-circuit television.

In thinking about this result, I realized that (for relativistic reasons) this sort of "nonlocal" connection across space implied a complementary connection across time. If we were seeing a genuine space-separated effect between people, then the same thing ought to work as a time-separated effect within one person. I called this proposed effect "presentiment" because the term suggests a response to a future emotional event.

I soon discovered that even the staunchest skeptics, those

ready to swear on a stack of scientific journals that psi was impossible, were somewhat less critical of intuitive hunches. That's because most people have had at least one.

I myself hardly believed the results of the studies I conducted on the magazine editor and others. But I couldn't find any mistakes in the study design or analysis of the results. Some months later, Dick Bierman, Ph.D., a professor at the University of Amsterdam, learned of my studies and couldn't believe them either. So he repeated the experiment in his lab and found the same results. Since then, two students of psychologist Robert Morris, Ph.D., at the University of Edinburgh, have also repeated the study, and again found similar results. More replication attempts are now under way in several other laboratories.

Not Absolute Proof

Do our experiments prove without question that the sixth sense exists? Not yet. What we have are three independent labs reporting similar effects based on data from more than 200 participants. The proof of the pudding will rest upon many more labs getting the same results. Still, our studies, combined with the outcomes of many other types of tests by dozens of investigators on precognition and other classes of psi phenomena, have caused even highly skeptical scientists to ponder what was previously unthinkable—the possibility of a genuine sixth sense.

In 1995, for example, no less an archskeptic than the late astronomer Carl Sagan rendered his lifelong opinion that all psi effects were impossible. But in one of his last books, *The Demon-Haunted World: Science as a Candle in the Dark*, he wrote, "At the time of writing there are three claims in the ESP field which, in my opinion, deserve serious study: (1) that by thought alone humans can (barely) affect random number generators in computers; (2) that people under mild sensory deprivation can receive thoughts or images "projected" at them; and (3) that young children sometimes report the details of a previous life, which upon checking turn out to be accurate and which they could not have known about in any other way than reincarnation."

ESP Could Change the World

If scientists eventually agree that a sixth sense exists, how might this change society? On one hand, it may change nothing; we may learn that genuine psi abilities are rare and only weakly predictive, and thus inconsequential for most practical purposes.

On the other hand, it's possible that the study of the sixth sense will revolutionize our understanding of causality and have radically new applications. For example, in the January issue of *Alternative Therapies*, psychologist William Braud, Ph.D., professor and research director at the Institute of Transpersonal Psychology and co-director of the Institute's William James Center for Consciousness Studies, discusses the concept of "retroactive intentional influence" as applied to healing. He poses the idea that in cases where serious illnesses disappear virtually overnight, perhaps a healer went back in time to jumpstart the healing process.

Braud is well aware of the mind-bending nature of this hypothesis, but it is not purely fantastical. In his article, he reviews several hundred experiments examining a wide range of retrocausal phenomena, from mental influence of random numbers generated by electronic circuits, to guessing picture targets selected in the future, to studies examining the "feeling of being stared at," to presentiment experiments. He concludes that this sizable but not well-known body of carefully controlled research indicates that some form of retroactive intentional influence is indeed possible, and may have important consequences for healing.

A less radical application might be for early warning systems. Imagine that on a future aircraft all the members of the flight crew are connected to an onboard computer system. The system is designed to continuously monitor heart rate, electrical activity in the skin, and blood flow. Before the crew comes aboard, each person is calibrated to see how he or she responds before, during and after different kinds of emotional and calm events. Each person's idiosyncratic responses are used to create a person-unique emotional "response template," which is fed into the computer.

While the plane is in the air, the computer monitors each crew member's body to assess their emotional level. If the computer detects that all crew members are about to have an emotional response (and the aircraft is otherwise operating normally), then the computer could alert the pilot. Sometimes even a few seconds of advance warning in an aircraft can save the lives of everyone on board.

Very likely, some intuitive hunches do indicate the presence of a sixth sense. But for whom? Probably everyone, to a degree. But just as some people have poor vision, it is also quite likely that some people are effectively "psi-blind." I suspect that in the future, with a little assistance from specialized technologies, the same way a hearing aid can improve poor hearing, it may become possible to boost our weak sixth sense.

Chapter 2

Fact or Fiction?

ESP Is Fiction

Ted Serios Is a Fraud

James Randi

Ted Serios was an obscure Chicago bellboy who appeared to have the mysterious ability to project his mental images onto film. This ability is called thoughtography by some people. It is said to be a form of ESP called psychokinesis. This means the ability to affect objects or organisms by mental power alone.

Serios became well known when a psychiatrist named Jule Eisenbud began testing him and ultimately wrote a book called *The World of Ted Serios*. But was Serios's ability genuine? Skeptics believe that Serios cheated: He used sleight of hand to make it appear that he had psychic powers.

The author of this article, James Randi, is a prominent skeptic of the paranormal. He's also a professional stage magician. Through his profession, he has learned many ways of making things appear to be different than they are in reality. He believes that Serios uses some of the same tricks stage magicians use, and he believes that the scientific studies of Serios are faulty.

Excerpted from *Flim-Flam: Psychics, ESP, Unicorns and Other Delusions*, by James Randi (Buffalo, NY: Prometheus Books, 1982). Copyright © 1982 by James Randi. Reprinted with permission.

Another *cause célèbre* that has faded away but made a big splash while it lasted was the "thoughtography" feat of Ted Serios, ex-bellboy turned "psychic," who discovered that by using a simple little device and gathering a few simple minds about him, he could work magic. Serios showed Dr. Jule Eisenbud, a Denver psychiatrist, that he could cause images to appear on the film of a borrowed and controlled Polaroid camera. For two years Eisenbud supported the Polaroid Corporation by purchasing vast quantities of film and having Serios make silly pictures. It was all described in a book by Eisenbud, *The World of Ted Serios*, which documents just how easily a psychiatrist can miss discovering his own delusions. In one episode Serios was asked to produce a picture of the *Thresher*, a nuclear submarine that had just been reported missing. Serios obliged, providing an image Eisenbud claimed actually *was* the *Thresher*, though in metaphorical form. To the untrained mind it *seemed* to be a photo of Queen Elizabeth II of England in her coronation robes, but that just shows how we ordinary folks can miss the great truths of science, not having the extensive training that would enable us to see beyond that mere superficiality. For, as Dr. Eisenbud shows, Queen Elizabeth is easily translated into the submarine.

Now it will be admitted that Liz has put on a few pounds in recent years, but her outline in no way resembles an atomic submarine. The doctor's proof is even more esoteric, as behooves a parapsychologist. Eisenbud explains that the Queen's name in Latin is Elizabeth Regina, and there we have half of it! What? You didn't see it? You'll *never* be a parapsychologist at this rate! Let's look at it again, shall we? ElizabeTH REgina. Is that better? Eisenbud's keen mind dis-

covered the initial four letters of THRESHER in the middle of
the Queen's Latin name! How clever of him. Being a
Freudian psychiatrist, he might be expected to drag Mom in
here somewhere—and he does. Queen Elizabeth is a
mother figure to millions. And the sea is the mother of all
life, it is said. The *Thresher* is in the sea. The French for
"mother" is *mère*. The French for "sea" is *mer*. Note that
these two words are similar. Ted Serios is attached to his
mother, and her name is—Esther! Isn't parapsychology just
grand, folks? For in the name Esther we have the SHER we
sought to complete THRESHER!

Serios has faded from the scene, though he was the darling
of the psi nuts for quite some time. *Fate* magazine tried to
give him a comeback a while ago, running an article with two
very fuzzy photos that it said were "psychically" produced by
Serios and that were supposed to show the then-fugitive Patty
Hearst with short-cropped hair. I have looked at those photos and I cannot see a person, let alone Patty. A few days after *Fate* hit the stands, Patty Hearst was apprehended. She had
long hair. A miss? No, of course not. The explanation given
for Serios's boo-boo was that his photos showed her as she
wanted to be. Or did I lose you somewhere?

How Serios Did It

Serios accomplished his wonders with a simple device that
is easily made. You will need a small, positive (magnifying)
lens, preferably about half an inch in diameter and with a
focal length of about one and a half inches. The latter can
be ascertained by measuring the distance between the lens
and the image of a distant object cast upon a piece of paper.
You'll need a small tube—as long as the focal length—to
hold the lens. From any color transparency (a thirty-five-
millimeter slide or a sixteen-millimeter motion picture
frame, for example) cut a circle that will fit onto one end of

the tube and attach it with glue. The lens is fitted to the other end.

You use the Serios gimmick by holding it in the hand with the lens end toward the palm. The victim—holding the Polaroid camera, which has been focused to infinity (distant)—is to snap the shutter when your hand is held before the lens. Keep the tube pointing straight into the camera. If it is off-center it will produce smeary pictures, as Serios did on many occasions. The photo that results is usually of poor but interesting quality. The pictures are often in the middle of a Polaroid frame, with a circular shape surrounded by black, as would be expected. If you like, you can be sure your device is not detected by placing a loose tube of paper around it. The device will slide out easily, and you can offer the paper tube for examination, though any parapsychologist will hesitate to look too carefully.

In 1967, writer Paul Welch had a piece on Serios in *Life* magazine that was totally supportive. The paper tube, which Serios called his "gismo" and which was used to conceal his optical device, was never mentioned. Although it was prominent in all of Serios's work, and showed up in most photos, *Life* chose to censor all reference to it to make a better story, for once the "gismo" was made known it would not be hard to figure out that the experimenters were allowing rather wide latitude for procedure in their "scientific tests."

But Eisenbud, leaping to the bait the "gismo" supplied, was quick to proclaim that though Serios *liked* to use the paper tube, he often *did not*, merely holding his hand there instead. When two photographers—Charles Reynolds and David Eisendrath—and Persi Diaconis, a prominent conjuring authority at Stanford University, went to Denver to see the super-psychic in action, they got the same old runaround. After one attempt, Serios quickly placed his hand in his pocket. Diaconis reached for it, trying to intercept the "gismo" before it could be emptied. Eisenbud threw himself between the two men and objected to this action, apparently forgetting that he had invited the three there to observe and that he was now interfering with that observation. A moment later, Serios produced the then-empty paper tube from his pocket for examination. A bit late.

Observers are invited to observe, but are blocked when they look too closely. . . .

Genuine Some of the Time?

Diaconis notes that at one point Dr. Eisenbud had asked of the observers, "If he's only genuine 10 percent of the time, isn't that enough for you guys?" No, it's not. For that 10 percent is well within the noise level of your very loose "experiments," doctor. In fact, a much higher percentage would still be within those very generous limits, given the expert observations of Reynolds, Eisendrath, and Diaconis. But we will admit that if the experiments had been done with good security and at least a brave attempt at proper control of the subject, 10 percent would be impressive. As it is, no one is impressed or satisfied.

Life chose not to say a word about the Reynolds-Eisendrath-Diaconis investigation, which had shown that the experiments they observed, contrary to what had been said by Eisenbud in his book, were "without adequate control over the essential materials" and revealed "irreparable methodological flaws in all phases of the experiments." *Life* was well aware of both the use of the giveaway "gismo" and the definitive report of the three competent observers, but in order to make a convincing case it ignored the contradictory evidence. When I questioned the magazine's staff about these omissions I was told that "an earlier draft of his [Welch's] story included mention of the 'gismo' struck out of the final version, as Serios does not *always* use it." True.

But a murderer does not kill *every* person he meets either. And what of the Reynolds-Eisendrath-Diaconis exposé? Nary a word from *Life* in response.

Eisenbud, demonstrating perfectly the irrationality of his kind, issued a challenge to me following the NBC "Today" show on which we had appeared with Serios and TV personality Hugh Downs. It was his inane idea that I submit to a preposterous set of controls—this after it had become quite plain to all investigators that his Trilby had been allowed to operate under the loosest and most incredible circumstances. I was to allow myself to be searched—including "a thorough inspection of body orifices"—and then "stripped, clad in a monkey suit, and sealed in a steel-walled, lead-lined, soundproof, windowless chamber." I had to be drunk as well. Then, I was to produce pictures. Why? Because Ted Serios operated under those conditions, said Eisenbud. Oh, yeah? When Reynolds, Eisendrath, and Diaconis were there, doctor, the security was so bad that not only was Serios allowed to wander in and out of the room, but Diaconis was able to switch a whole batch of film *right under your nose*, and you never even knew it! And I have all three witnesses (sober, and not in monkey suits).

If this great investigator and peerless observer required Serios to perform under the conditions he outlined for me, why didn't he mention it earlier? I refer the curious to the *Journal of the American Society for Psychical Research (JASPR)*. In that publication Eisenbud wrote thousands of words about his experiments with Serios, referring many times to tests wherein sealed rooms were used, lead glass was employed, and the camera was kept isolated from Serios. I would like to know where in these accounts is mentioned a test of the kind he claims to have performed. It simply does not exist. Also nonexistent are the powers of Serios and the objectivity of those who investigated him.

Gullible Researcher

Dr. Eisenbud is at his best when he writes for the parapsychology journals. There he can throw around terminology that obfuscates the basic facts beautifully. In the July 1967 issue of the *JASPR*, Eisenbud and his associates damn themselves with their own pens. Here they discuss the "gismo" and mention that without it Serios obtains results "no different from the results he gets with its use." They then proceed to describe a "target" attempt in March 1965 in which Serios achieved wonderful things. All six "associates" suggested targets, and Dr. Johann R. Marx suggested a World War I aircraft. Serios and Dr. Marx had spent much time discussing early aircraft, a subject of great interest to both men, and I am not surprised to discover that Serios came along that evening, knowing that Marx would be there, equipped with an appropriately prepared gimmick for the occasion. Eisenbud carefully points out that Serios, during that session, sometimes used the gimmick and sometimes did not, and produced five prints, all bearing pictures of the same general object—part of a vintage plane.

Early in the *JASPR* piece Eisenbud compounds his naïveté by saying of the "gismo" that "indeed, no other reason [than to aid in concentration] for its existence or use has yet been discovered." If Eisenbud had looked at his data carefully, as I did, he'd have seen that a use just might suggest itself, because Serios produced pictures *only* on trial numbers 15, 20, 22, 26, and 33—*the only five during which he used the "gismo."*

To this day, so I'm told, Eisenbud believes that a bellboy from Chicago could imprint pictures on film by miraculous means. His ego simply does not permit him to realize that he was duped, and he will carry his delusions with him to the grave. Perhaps Dr. Börje Löfgren, writing in the *Journal of the American Psychoanalytic Association*, had it right when he described Eisenbud and other parapsychology enthusiasts as "decaying minds" with "thinking defects and disturbed relations to reality." At the very least, it seems that Dr. Eisenbud is not rowing with both oars in the water. [*Editor's note:* This article was published in 1982; Eisenbud died in 1999.]

Bad Research

Statistician Persi Diaconis, whom I have known for many years (since his early interest in conjuring), is in a particularly strong position from which to judge the value of parapsychological claims. His knowledge of sleight of hand and mentalism is second to none, and I do not make that statement lightly. Persi is capable of miracles with a deck of cards that would put to shame many a professional magician, and his awareness of the psychological subtleties of the conjurer equip him perfectly for such investigations. Unhappily for the art, Mr. Diaconis long ago chose a more serious profession and today is involved in heady statistical problems. His help as a consultant has greatly assisted my work, and though he has withdrawn from active participation in the CSICOP [Committee for the Scientific Investigation of Claims of the Paranormal], he contributes to our efforts when he can spare the time.

A recent paper of his, published in *Science*, the journal of the American Association for the Advancement of Science, stirred up quite a few para-scientists who were castigated in the article. Diaconis correctly pointed out that "modern parapsychological research *is* important . . . [but] poorly designed, badly run, and inappropriately analyzed experiments seem to be an even greater obstacle in the field than subject cheating. . . . There always seem to be many loopholes and loose ends. The same mistakes are made again and again." It stands to reason that if either subject cheating or bad experimental procedure can damn the work of a parapsychologist, then a combination of both these elements double-damns it.

Diaconis has long been examining parapsychological work, not as a passive observer but as an involved investigator. In addition to having been one of the experts called in to examine the Serios-Eisenbud episode, he has been close to the work of Charles Tart, prominent parapsychologist. The case of "B.D.," a card-trick artist who fooled the paranormalists, fell apart under Diaconis's examination.

But of course, there are always examples of these wonders that he cannot get access to, because of the secrecy that often surrounds them, the unwillingness of the investigators to reveal important details of the experiments, or simply the barriers of time and distance. "I have certainly read and been told about events that I cannot explain," says Diaconis. I must of course admit the same thing. I also very much agree with his judgment in another statement he has made: "I have been able to have direct experience with more than a dozen experiments and detailed second-hand knowledge about perhaps twenty more. In every case the details of what actually transpired prevent the experiment from being considered seriously as evidence for paranormal phenomena."

Russian Psychics Exposed

Massimo Polidoro

During the 1960s and 1970s word leaked out that scientists in the Soviet Union were studying paranormal phenomena—and were finding impressive evidence supporting it. In particular, several Soviet psychics were said to be able to perform amazing feats of psychokinesis—affecting objects with one's mind alone. They were said to be able to move objects, suspend objects in the air, even affect human body workings, all through mental power. Gradually, reports and videotapes showing these psychics in action were smuggled to the West. Scientists studied the evidence, and many were impressed. However, some thought the impressive Soviet activities were mere trickery. In the following article, the author, Massimo Polidoro, comments on three Soviet psychics and their apparent use of standard magician tricks. Polidoro is cofounder and director of CICAP, the Italian Committee for the Investigation of Claims of the Paranormal. He has written several books dealing with the paranormal.

From "Secrets of a Russian Psychic," by Massimo Polidoro, *Skeptical Inquirer*, July/August 1997. Copyright © 1997 by *Skeptical Inquirer*. Reprinted with permission.

For years, psychic research in the USSR, owing to the aura of secrecy that surrounded it, has been regarded as some kind of myth. It was being said, for example, that the Russians were far ahead in parapsychological discoveries and that the West had better invest lots of money in the field to avoid a "psi-gap." The sparse information that reached the West hinted to extraordinary faculties being scientifically demonstrated by amazing psychics. During the early 1960s, interest in Soviet paranormal claims was first aroused by newspaper articles describing the astonishing abilities of Rosa Kuleshova, a twenty-two-year-old Russian girl who apparently could read print while blindfolded (*Time*, January 25, 1963; *Life*, June 12, 1964). However, the loose conditions in which Rosa operated allowed for very easy methods of deception to be used.

In 1968, films showing Nina Kulagina apparently moving objects with her mind (psychokinesis, or PK) were viewed at the First Moscow International Conference on Parapsychology and were also observed by some Western scientists. Finally, the general public became aware of the varied work in parapsychology carried out in the USSR with the publication of Sheila Ostrander and Lynn Schroeder's *Psychic Discoveries Behind the Iron Curtain* (1970), followed by various other similar publications on the subject.

Many films of Russian psychics at work have now been seen on Western TV shows and documentaries. The most popular are those that show apparent PK in action. We have seen, then, Nina Kulagina apparently moving compass needles and light objects, Boris Ermolaev "levitating" small objects, and Alla Vinogradova willing round objects to roll on flat surfaces.

Russian PK Stars

As for Nina Kulagina, the conditions under which she operated were far from acceptable by basic scientific standards. Tests were frequently carried out at her own home or in hotel rooms; no tight controls were ever applied, owing in part to the fact that a demonstration might take several hours of preparation (i.e., concentration by Nina), which, of course, was no guarantee of success. Also, when watching these films, anybody who has a background in magic cannot avoid the feeling that she is using standard conjuring techniques: magnets hidden on her body to move the compass needle; threads or thin hair to move objects across the table; small mirrors concealed in her hand to read signs with numbers and letters being held behind her. Unfortunately, no expert in conjuring techniques was ever present at Kulagina's demonstrations.

Boris Ermolaev, a Russian film director, became relatively famous during the 1970s for his apparent ability to suspend objects in midair by concentrating on them. Ermolaev didn't perform on stage but showed his demonstrations *"only to serious scientists of his own choosing or to close friends"* (italics mine). He and others were tested by Professor Venyamin Pushkin, who stated: "The experiments were conducted under the strictest controls, and no devices of any kind were used." However, in a 1992 *World of Discovery* documentary called "Secrets of the Russian Psychics," Ermolaev's method was finally revealed. He used to sit on a chair and then place the objects to be suspended between his knees; unfortunately for him, the light conditions when the documentary crew was filming were probably not what he was accustomed to. That's how the TV crew was able to capture a fine thread fixed at both his knees to which he attached the objects; the whole unmasking procedure was filmed and shown during the documentary.

Alla Vinogradova is another story.

Vinogradova's Moving Objects

A child psychologist and teacher, wife of Russian psi-researcher Victor Adamenko, Alla Vinogradova saw in 1969 a film of Kulagina in action and suspected that she too could move objects without touching them. In fact, trained by Adamenko, she discovered she could really move objects placed on transparent surfaces. Films of her demonstrations were shot in the early 1970s, and recently the previously mentioned *World of Discovery* documentary on Russian psychics had an interesting section devoted to her. Here she was presented as she is today, still demonstrating the same abilities for the camera. She took such objects as cigarettes, aluminum cigar tubes, and pens and put them on a Plexiglass plate suspended between two chairs; in such conditions she was able to make them rotate, roll, and move just by having her hand approach, but never touch, them. The demonstration was quite puzzling. It did appear very natural and repeatable and it seemed that the usual tricks (like secretly blowing on the surface to have the object move thanks to the air current thus created) were unlikely.

Some time ago, I visited [magician and psi debunker] James Randi in Florida; he had recently returned from Russia, where he had gone for some filming to be included in *Nova's* 1993 documentary about his work: "Secrets of the Psychics." Randi told me that, while he was there, the TV production staff approached Vinogradova and asked if she would agree to demonstrate her abilities on camera. She agreed; however, she put forth the condition that Randi had to be kept away from the room where filming was to take place. This was quite an inappropriate request, considering that the documentary was dedicated to Randi's investigations. Nonetheless, Randi accepted her veto: this way, she would present her demonstration as she always did, that is, not under controlled conditions. It was, in any event, an occasion to film her from different angles and to have better video material for study.

The segments filmed with Vinogradova were not included in the final documentary; however, Randi had copies of the original unedited footage that he was going to show me. Vinogradova was seen speaking, in Russian, with the operators, then walking back and forth on the thick carpet, combing her hair, and rubbing with a towel the surface of a Plexiglass plate placed on top of four glasses turned upside down on a table. Originally, she started to demonstrate her abilities with various objects: cigarettes, pens, plastic rings, a small wooden doll from a set of nesting dolls, a small hairspray bottle, and a glass. All objects moved quite freely, as seen in the other films; only the spray bottle and the glass, being the heaviest objects, moved little or only wobbled back and forth as she passed her hand over them. Suddenly, while moving the nesting doll, a white thread that was on the table, under the Plexiglass, was seen to be moving too, following the doll. I pointed this out to Randi and he told me that the cameraman, after shooting the film, told him that he had seen the moving thread but didn't realize that he had actually zoomed in on it and caught it on film. Randi himself hadn't yet had a chance to examine the film so he was quite interested too. "That thread," he told me, "was from the torn end of a cloth-based duct tape used to hold tiny microphones to the edge of the Plexiglass. The microphones were there to detect if she was doing any blowing to move the objects. The thread was not placed there purposely. It was just a loose thread. But, of course, it proved to be the indicator needed."

A Neglected Explanation?

Randi and I discussed the possibility of static electricity being solely responsible for the phenomena. In the *World of Discovery* documentary, this possibility was mentioned as an explanation proposed by skeptics, but it was immediately discarded since Vinogradova said she could move objects weighing up to two hundred grams. She claimed that it was impossible to do this using only static electricity. We thought we should try to repeat her performance with a Plexiglass plate, but, owing to other things we were involved with at the time, we didn't have a chance to get around to it before my departure.

Once back in Italy, I discussed the subject with my colleagues Luigi Garlaschelli and Franco Ramaccini of CICAP (the Italian Committee for the Investigation of Claims of the Paranormal) and soon we tested the theory of static electricity. Ramaccini found a Plexiglass plate and showed us how easy it was to move any kind of round object on top of it, only by making use of the repelling forces caused by static electricity. Of course, the effect was quite better if the surface was electrically charged, by rubbing a towel on it. Heavier objects, like glasses and spray bottles, could be as easily moved. Everything shown on Alla Vinogradova's films, then, now seemed to have a very simple and rational explanation.

We then wondered whether others had already discovered this very interesting and counterintuitive phenomenon. No trace or mention of Vinogradova's abilities appeared in the skeptical literature on the paranormal or in popular science "magic" books, and some of the best-known skeptics didn't know much about her.

I then got in touch with today's leading parapsychologists and was more than pleased to discover that they had a lot of information on Vinogradova and, above all, had solved the mystery years ago.

The Help of Parapsychologists

Stanley Krippner, psychologist at Saybrook Institute in San Francisco and past president of the Parapsychological Association, told me that he had dealt with Vinogradova in his book *Human Possibilities* (1980). In it he writes that, when he was in Russia, he observed Vinogradova in action with an aluminum tube: "She picked it up and rubbed it for a few seconds—suggesting to me that she was simply producing an electrostatic charge that would cause her hand to repel the tube. As expected, the object moved across the table." He was able to reproduce the effect once back in the United States. In his book, Krippner quotes a Canadian parapsychologist, A.R.G. Owen, who back in 1975 wrote, "Anyone can produce this effect. . . . It is entirely due to static electricity."

Richard Broughton, director of the Rhine Research Center in Durham, North Carolina, explained to me that: "Adamenko had a notion that he could 'train' people to produce Kulagina-like effects by starting them out moving objects by static electricity, and then gradually moving them to objects that would not be susceptible to static electricity effects."

A Lesson to Be Learned

Although the more impressive feat of moving objects not susceptible to static electricity hasn't so far been publicly demonstrated by Vinogradova or others, I think there's a lesson to be learned. Serious skeptics and serious parapsychologists should establish more occasions for mutual cooperation. Parapsychologists shouldn't be generally thought of by skeptics as more gullible than other researchers (although there have been many examples of such cases) simply because they may have a more open attitude toward psi. Some of the best skeptical investigations in early psychical research were carried out by members of the Society for Psychical Research. More important, however, is the fact that today parapsychologists are quite aware of the pitfalls of experimenting with self-proclaimed psychics, and they either make use of experts in psychic fraud or, like Richard Wiseman of the Perrot-Warrick Research Unit at the University of Hertfordshire, England, have themselves developed an expertise in this field.

I hope the era of hard fights between proponents and critics of parapsychology is over. The time has come for a new era of cooperation, where there may be agreement on some basic points, namely, that it is in both sides' interest to get rid of superstition and charlatans, and also that it is in both sides' interest to examine the claims, rather than simply argue over them. I am not saying that there may be real psi to be discovered, but, at least, that there may be something interesting to be discovered about human psychology.

"Psychics" Simulate ESP by Cold Reading

Ray Hyman

Whether or not you believe in psychic abilities, there have probably been times when you have been impressed by the apparent mind-reading skill of a stage magician, a fortune-teller, or a psychic. How do these people do it? How do they know so much about a stranger? The author of the following article, Ray Hyman, says that many of them do it not with ESP but by using a technique called "cold reading." The psychic or mind reader fools the audience by using common skills, including close observation, vagueness, and a projection of confidence. As you read the following article, you will see that you unconsciously use some cold-reading skills yourself.

Hyman is a long-time professor of psychology and an amateur magician. He is a well-known critic of paranormal claims.

Excerpted from "'Cold Reading': How to Convince Strangers That You Know All About Them," by Ray Hyman, *The Outer Edge: Classic Investigations of the Paranormal*, edited by Joe Nickell, Barry Karr, and Tom Genoni (Amherst, NY: Committee for the Scientific Investigation of Claims of the Paranormal, 1996). Copyright © 1996 by Committee for the Scientific Investigation of Claims of the Paranormal. Reprinted with permission.

"Cold reading" is a procedure by which a "reader" is able to persuade a client whom he has never before met that he knows all about the client's personality and problems. At one extreme this can be accomplished by delivering a stock spiel, or "psychological reading," that consists of highly general statements that can fit any individual. A reader who relies on psychological readings will usually have memorized a set of stock spiels. He then can select a reading to deliver that is relatively more appropriate to the general category that the client fits—a young unmarried girl, a senior citizen, and so on. Such an attempt to fit the reading to the client makes the psychological reading a closer approximation to the true cold reading.

The cold reading, at its best, provides the client with a character assessment that is uniquely tailored to fit him or her. The reader begins with the same assumptions that guide the psychological reader who relies on the stock spiel. These assumptions are (1) that we all are basically more alike than different; (2) that our problems are generated by the same major transitions of birth, puberty, work, marriage, children, old age, and death; (3) that, with the exception of curiosity seekers and troublemakers, people come to a character reader because they need someone to listen to their conflicts involving love, money, and health. The cold reader goes beyond these common denominators by gathering as much additional information about the client as possible. Sometimes such information is obtained in advance of the reading. If the reading is through appointment, the reader can use directories and other sources to gather information. When the client enters the consulting room, an assistant can examine the coat left behind (and often the purse as well) for papers, notes, labels, and other such cues about socioeconomic status, and so on. Most cold readers, however, do not need such advance information.

Good Memory and Astute Observation

The cold reader basically relies on a good memory and acute observation. The client is carefully studied. The clothing—for example, style, neatness, cost, age—provides a host of cues for helping the reader make shrewd guesses about socioeconomic level, conservatism or extroversion, and other characteristics. The client's physical features—weight, posture, looks, eyes, and hands provide further cues. The hands are especially revealing to the good reader. The manner of speech, use of grammar, gestures, and eye contact are also good sources. To the good reader the huge amount of information coming from an initial sizing-up of the client greatly narrows the possible categories into which he classifies clients. His knowledge of actuarial and statistical data about various subcultures in the population already provides him the basis for making an uncanny and strikingly accurate assessment of the client.

But the skilled reader can go much further in particularizing his reading. He wants to zero in as quickly as possible on the precise problem that is bothering the client. On the basis of his initial assessment he makes some tentative hypotheses. He tests these out by beginning his assessment in general terms, touching upon general categories of problems and watching the reaction of the client. If he is on the wrong track the client's reactions—eye movements, pupillary dilation, other bodily mannerisms—will warn him. When he is on the right track other reactions will tell him so. By watching the client's reactions as he tests out different hypotheses during his spiel, the good reader quickly hits upon what is bothering the customer and begins to adjust the reading to the situation. By this time, the client has usually been persuaded that the reader, by some uncanny means, has gained insights into the client's innermost thoughts. His guard is now down. Often he opens up and actually tells the reader, who is also a good listener, the details of his situation. The reader, after a suitable interval, will usually feed back the information that the client has given him in such a way that the client will be further amazed at how much the reader "knows" about him. Invariably the client leaves the reader without realizing that everything he has been told is simply what he himself has unwittingly revealed to the reader.

The Stock Spiel

The preceding paragraphs indicate that the cold reader is a highly skilled and talented individual. And this is true. But what is amazing about this area of human assessment is how successfully even an unskilled and incompetent reader can persuade a client that he has fathomed the client's true nature. It is probably a tribute to the creativeness of the human mind that a client can, under the right circumstances, make sense out of almost any reading and manage to fit it to his own unique situation. All that is necessary is that the reader make out a plausible case for why the reading ought to fit. The client will do the rest.

You can achieve a surprisingly high degree of success as a character reader even if you merely use a stock spiel which you give to every client. [Psychologist N.D.] Sundberg, for example, found that if you deliver the following character sketch to a college male, he will usually accept it as a reasonably accurate description of himself: "You are a person who is very normal in his attitudes, behavior and relationships with people. You get along well without effort. People naturally like you and you are not overly critical of them or yourself. You are neither overly conventional nor overly in-dividualistic. Your prevailing mood is one of optimism and constructive effort, and you are not troubled by periods of depression, psychosomatic illness or nervous symptoms."

Sundberg found that the college female will respond with even more pleasure to the following sketch: "You ap-pear to be a cheerful, well-balanced person. You may have some alternation of happy and unhappy moods, but they are not extreme now. You have few or no problems with your health. You are sociable and mix well with others. You are adaptable to social situations. You tend to be adventur-ous. Your interests are wide. You are fairly self-confident and usually think clearly."

A Generic Personality Sketch

Sundberg conducted his study over [fifty] years ago. But the sketches still work well today. Either will tend to work well with both sexes. More recently, several laboratory studies have had excellent success with the following stock spiel:

> Some of your aspirations tend to be pretty unrealistic. At times you are extroverted, affable, sociable, while at other times you are introverted, wary and reserved. You have found it unwise to be too frank in revealing yourself to oth-ers. You pride yourself on being an independent thinker and do not accept others' opinions without satisfactory proof. You prefer a certain amount of change and variety and be-come dissatisfied when hemmed in by restrictions and lim-itations. At times you have serious doubts as to whether you have made the right decision or done the right thing. Disci-plined and controlled on the outside, you tend to be worri-some and insecure on the inside.

> Your sexual adjustment has presented some problems for you. While you have some personality weaknesses, you are generally able to compensate for them. You have a great deal of unused capacity which you have not turned to your ad-vantage. You have a tendency to be critical of yourself. You

have a strong need for other people to like you and for them to admire you.

Interestingly enough the statements in this stock spiel were first used in 1948 by [psychologist] Bertram Forer in a classroom demonstration of personal validation. He obtained most of them from a newsstand astrology book. Forer's students, who thought the sketch was uniquely intended for them as a result of a personality test, gave the sketch an average rating of 4.26 on a scale of 0 (poor) to 5 (perfect). As many as 16 out of his 39 students (41 percent) rated it as a perfect fit to their personality. Only five gave it a rating below 4 (the worst being a rating of 2, meaning "average"). Almost 30 years later students give the same sketch an almost identical rating as a unique description of themselves.

The Technique in Action

The acceptability of the stock spiel depends upon the method and circumstances of its delivery. As we shall later see, laboratory studies have isolated many of the factors that contribute to persuading clients that the sketch is a unique description of themselves. A great deal of the success of the spiel depends upon "setting the stage." The reader tries to persuade the client that the sketch is tailored especially for him or her. The reader also creates the impression that it is based on a reliable and proven assessment procedure. The way the sketch is delivered and dramatized also helps. And many of the rules that I give for the cold reading also apply to the delivery of the stock spiel.

The stock spiel, when properly delivered, can be quite effective. In fact, with the right combination of circumstances the stock spiel is often accepted as a perfect and unique description by the client. But, in general, one can achieve even greater success as a character analyst if one uses the more flexible technique of the cold reader. In this method one plays a sort of detective role in which one takes on the role of a Sherlock Holmes. (See the "Case of the Cardboard Box" for an excellent example of cold reading.) One observes the jewelry, prices the clothing, evaluates the speech mannerisms, and studies the reactions of the subject. Then whatever information these observations provide is pieced together into a character reading which is aimed more specifically at the particular client.

"Amazing Insight"

A good illustration of the cold reader in action occurs in a story told by the well-known magician John Mulholland. The incident took place in the 1930s. A young lady in her late twenties or early thirties visited a character reader. She was wearing expensive jewelry, a wedding band, and a black dress of cheap material. The observant reader noted that she was wearing shoes which were currently being advertised for people with foot trouble. (Pause at this point and imagine that you are the reader; see what you would make of these clues.)

By means of just these observations the reader proceeded to amaze his client with his insights. He assumed that this client came to see him, as did most of his female customers, because of a love or financial problem. The black dress and the wedding band led him to reason that her husband had died recently. The expensive jewelry suggested that she had been financially comfortable during marriage, but the cheap dress indicated that her husband's death had left her penniless. The therapeutic shoes signified that she was now standing on her feet more than she was used to, implying that she was working to support herself since her husband's death.

The reader's shrewdness led him to the following conclusion—which turned out to be correct: The lady had met a man who had proposed to her. She wanted to marry the man to end her economic hardship. But she felt guilty about marrying so soon after her husband's death. The reader told her what she had come to hear—that it was all right to marry without further delay.

The Rules of the Game

Whether you prefer to use the formula reading or to employ the more flexible technique of the cold reader, the following bits of advice will help to contribute to your success as a character reader.

1. *Remember that the key ingredient of a successful character reading is confidence.* If you look and act as if you believe in what you are doing, you will be able to sell even a bad reading to most of your subjects.

The laboratory studies support this rule. Many readings are accepted as accurate because the statements do fit most people. But even readings that would ordinarily be rejected as inaccurate will be accepted if the reader is viewed as a person with prestige or as someone who knows what he is doing.

One danger of playing the role of reader is that you will persuade yourself that you really are divining true character. This happened to me. I started reading palms when I was in my teens as a way to supplement my income from doing magic and mental shows. When I started I did not believe in palmistry. But I knew that to "sell" it I had to act as if I did. After a few years I became a firm believer in palmistry. One day the late Dr. Stanley Saks, who was a professional mentalist and a man I respected, tactfully suggested that it would make an interesting experiment if I deliberately gave readings opposite to what the lines indicated. I tried this out with a few clients. To my surprise and horror my readings were just as successful as ever. Ever since then I have been interested in the powerful forces that convince us, reader and client alike, that something is so when it really isn't.

Creativity Helps

2. *Make creative use of the latest statistical abstracts, polls, and surveys.* This can provide you with a wealth of material about what various subclasses of our society believe, do, want, worry about, and so on. For example, if you can ascertain about a client such things as the part of the country he comes from, the size of the city he was brought up in, his parents' religion and vocations, his educational level and age, you already are in possession of information that should enable you to predict with high probability his voting preferences, his beliefs on many issues, and other traits.

3. *Set the stage for your reading.* Profess a modesty about your talents. Make no excessive claims. This catches your subject off guard. You are not challenging him to a battle of wits. You can read his character; whether he cares to believe you or not is his concern.

4. *Gain his cooperation in advance.* Emphasize that the success of the reading depends as much upon his sincere cooperation as upon your efforts. (After all, you imply, you already have a successful career at reading characters. You are not on trial—he is.) State that due to difficulties of language and communication, you may not always convey the exact meaning which you intend. In these cases he is to strive to reinterpret the message in terms of his own vocabulary and life.

You accomplish two invaluable ends with this dodge. You have an alibi in case the reading doesn't click; it's his fault not yours! And your subject will strive to fit your generalities to his specific life occurrences. Later, when he recalls the reading he will recall it in terms of specifics; thus you gain credit for much more than you actually said.

Of all the pieces of advice this is the most crucial. To the extent that the client is made an active participant in the reading the reading will succeed. The good reader, deliberately or unwittingly, is the one who forces the client to actively search his memory to make sense of the reader's statements.

Use a Gimmick

5. *Use a gimmick such as a crystal ball, tarot cards, or palm reading.* The use of palmistry, say, serves two useful purposes. It lends an air of novelty to the reading; but, more important, it serves as a cover for you to stall and to formulate your next statement. While you are trying to think of something to say next, you are apparently carefully studying a new wrinkle or line in the hand. Holding hands, in addition to any emotional thrills you may give or receive thereby, is another good way of detecting the reactions of the subject to what you are saying (the principle is the same as "muscle reading").

It helps, in the case of palmistry or other gimmicks, to study some manuals so that you know roughly what the various diagnostic signs are supposed to mean. A clever way of using such gimmicks to pin down a client's problem is to use a variant of "Twenty Questions," somewhat like this: Tell the client you have only a limited amount of time for the reading. You could focus on the heart line, which deals with emotional entanglements; on the fate line, which deals with vocational pursuits and money matters; the head line, which deals with personal problems; the health line, and so on. Ask him or her which one to focus on first. This quickly pins down the major category of problem on the client's mind.

6. *Have a list of stock phrases at the tip of your tongue.* Even if you are doing a cold reading, the liberal sprinkling of stock phrases amidst your regular reading will add body to the reading and will fill in time as you try to formulate more precise characterizations. You can use the statements in the preceding stock spiels as a start. Memorize a few of them before undertaking your initial ventures into character reading. Palmisty, tarot, and other fortune-telling manuals also

are rich sources for good phrases.

7. *Keep your eyes open.* Also use your other senses. We have seen how to size up the client on the basis of clothing, jewelry, mannerisms, and speech. Even a crude classification on such a basis can provide sufficient information for a good reading. Watch the impact of your statements upon the subject. Very quickly you will learn when you are "hitting home" and when you are "missing the boat."

8. *Use the technique of "fishing."* This is simply a device for getting the subject to tell you about himself. Then you rephrase what he has told you into a coherent sketch and feed it back to him. One version of fishing is to phrase each statement in the form of a question. Then wait for the subject to reply (or react). If the reaction is positive, then the reader turns the statement into a positive assertion. Often the subject will respond by answering the implied question and then some. Later he will tend to forget that he was the source of your information. By making your statements into questions you also force the subject to search through his memory to retrieve specific instances to fit your general statement.

9. *Learn to be a good listener.* During the course of a reading your client will be bursting to talk about incidents that are brought up. The good reader allows the client to talk at will. On one occasion I observed a tea-leaf reader. The client actually spent 75 percent of the total time talking. Afterward when I questioned the client about the reading she vehemently insisted that she had not uttered a single word during the course of the reading. The client praised the reader for having so astutely told her what in fact she herself had spoken.

Another value of listening is that most clients who seek the services of a reader actually want someone to listen to their problems. In addition many clients have already made up their minds about what choices they are going to make. They merely want support to carry out their decision.

10. *Dramatize your reading.* Give back what little information you do have or pick up a little bit at a time. Make it seem more than it is. Build word pictures around each divulgence. Don't be afraid of hamming it up.

An Air of Mystery

11. *Always give the impression that you know more than you are saying.* The successful reader, like the family doctor, always acts as if he knows much more. Once you persuade the client that you know one item of information about him that you could not possibly have obtained through normal channels, the client will automatically assume you know all. At this point he will typically open up and confide in you.

12. *Don't be afraid to flatter your subject every chance you get.* An occasional subject will protest such flattery, but will still cherish it. In such cases you can further flatter him by saying, "You are always suspicious of people who flatter you. You just can't believe that someone will say good of you unless he is trying to achieve some ulterior goal."

13. *Finally remember the golden rule: Tell the client what he wants to hear.* Sigmund Freud once made an astute observation. He had a client who had been to a fortune-teller many years previously. The fortune-teller had predicted that she would have twins. Actually she never had children. Yet, despite the fact that the reader had been wrong, the client still spoke of her in glowing terms. Freud tried to figure out why this was so. He finally concluded that at the time of the original reading the client wanted desperately to have children. The fortune-teller sensed this and told her what she wanted to hear. From this Freud inferred that the successful fortune-teller is one who predicts what the client secretly wishes to happen rather than what actuary will happen.

Christians Should Not Fool Around with ESP

Doug Trouten

Some people consider ESP to be an extension of normal human abilities, but others think that ESP and other paranormal abilities are occult—that is, they may involve some supernatural power. Consequently, some religious groups are wary of exploring this topic. In the following article, Doug Trouten explores some Christian concerns about ESP. Trouten is president of the Evangelical Press Association, an organization whose members are involved in evangelical Christian publishing.

Pick any number from one to 10. Multiply by nine. If the result is a two-digit number, add the digits together. Got it? Good. Now subtract five, and choose the letter from the alphabet that corresponds with the result (one is "a," two is "b," and so on). Finally, choose a country whose name begins with your chosen letter, and concentrate on the name of that country.

Wait—I'm picking up a strong impression here. Are you thinking of Denmark?

What you've just experienced could seem like a display of psychic powers, but it's really a simple trick. Still, with tricks no more sophisticated than this one, so-called psychics are raking in huge profits from gullible people who are looking for answers and a touch of the super natural.

The occult has long been part of our culture, but today we're seeing increased acceptance of "occult lite." Movies like *The Sixth Sense* and television programs like "The Others" reinforce beliefs in the paranormal. Astrology columns are published daily in respectable newspapers. Tarot card readers set up shop in shopping malls. And psychics are just a phone call away—at $4.99 per minute.

Psychic phenomena have become so mainstream that the New York City Human Resources Administration started a program to give welfare recipients training as psychics to get them off public assistance. (The Psychic Network paid "workfare" recipients $10 per hour after they received training through the city. Applicants needed only a high-school diploma and the ability to read and speak English. At least 15 welfare clients passed a class in Tarot card reading and were hired by the company before a report in *The New York Times* forced the cancellation of the program.)

The biggest telephone psychic operation, Psychic Friends, was taking in $150 million per year before it went bankrupt, done in by fierce competition from many smaller companies. (Shouldn't they have seen it coming?)

Buoyed by high-tech infomercials and computerized billing connected to 900-numbers, the telephone psychic industry is estimated to reach $1.4 billion in 2000, up from $670 million in 1994, according to *Telemedia News & Views*.

Is It Real?

Though seekers may be tempted to believe that their "psychic friends" have real powers, ask yourself this: If you had the ability to see the future, would you spend your day talking on the phone with strangers for 20 to 25 cents per minute (the typical wage for a phone psychic)? Or would you spend your time buying lottery tickets and playing the stock market? If there really are people out there with psychic abilities, they're probably not waiting for you to call.

The big name psychics are no better. Supermarket tabloids are filled with psychic predictions by top psychics, but few—if any—ever come true. For instance, psychic predictions for 1999 included O.J. Simpson confessing to murder, Wynona Judd quitting country music to become a woman wrestler, the Statue of Liberty losing both arms in a terrorist blast, and marijuana replacing petroleum as the nation's fuel of choice. Nobody predicted the massive earthquake in Turkey or the death of John F. Kennedy, Jr.

Many paranormal practitioners—from astrologers to palm readers—rely on a psychological principle known as the "Barnum effect," which states that people tend to accept vague and general personality descriptions as uniquely applicable to themselves without realizing that the same description could be applied to just about anyone.

In a classic experiment, psychologist R.R. Forer gave a personality test to students, ignored their answers, and gave each one the same analysis:

"You have a need for other people to like and admire you, and yet you tend to be critical of yourself. . . . You have considerable unused capacity that you have not turned to your advantage. . . . At times you have serious doubts as to whether you have made the right decision or done the right thing. You prefer a certain amount of change and variety and become dissatisfied when hemmed in by restrictions and limitations. . . . At times you are extroverted, affable, and sociable, while at other times you are introverted, wary, and reserved."

Student evaluations of this personality assessment ranged from "good" to "excellent." Most people are so narcissistic that they don't want to believe how much they have in common with everyone else. Charlatans use this psychological principle to make gullible people believe they have psychic powers.

Other fakers use simple magic tricks. Recent televised specials featuring street magician David Blaine showed spectators ready to ascribe supernatural power to Blaine in response to card tricks.

Is There a Darker Side?

Tal Brooke, head of Spiritual Counterfeits Project (www.scp-inc.org), believes there is a demonic reality to some psychic phenomenon.

"In the Book of Acts we see a girl with a soothsaying spirit who followed an apostle around," Brooke says. "He rebuked her and the spirit because it was trafficking in the supernatural and trying to credit to God that which was coming from dark forces. We can go back to Moses and the court of Pharaoh and see supernatural events that were not of God. We do not have an impotent devil or impotent demons. They can do things within range. The biblical view is that it's not just a three-dimensional universe—that there's much more going on."

Christian illusionist Andre Kole disagrees. While some psychics may believe they are gifted and others use trickery, Kole says both groups have complete lack of psychic power.

"I've investigated this all over the world and have not

found any genuine phenomenon presented by anyone in the occult, Satanism, or witchcraft," says Kole. "I back up my statements with a $25,000 challenge to anyone who's involved in any of these things and can demonstrate a true supernatural power. In 35 years, no one anywhere in the world has even been able to pass a preliminary test."

Kole, who is recognized as one of the magic world's leading inventors and works with top magicians such as David Copperfield, is uniquely qualified to uncover phony psychics because of his vast knowledge of magicians' methods.

Though many Christians believe some psychics get their information from demons, Kole disagrees.

"People used to say that Jeanne Dixon got her information from demons," he explains. "Well, with all of the prophecies she missed, if she was possessed by demons, it was a dumb bunch of demons."

Kole says it's a mistake to ascribe supernatural power even to demonic forces. "For Christians this is important because the apologetic argument that Jesus used was a miracle. Jesus said if you have a hard time believing in me, believe because of the miracles. We are undermining Jesus' miracles when we suggest that anybody else has true supernatural powers."

Terry Howell, who pastors Heartland Community Church in Medina, Ohio, was director of research for Kole from 1987–1996. He says that because Christians know there is a supernatural world, we have a tendency to see supernatural power where none exists.

"If we don't understand it, we have a tendency to say that it's super natural," he says. "My belief is that if you don't understand it, it simply means that you don't understand it."

Richard Howe, associate professor of philosophy and apologetics at Southern Evangelical Seminary in North Carolina, takes a middle view.

"The large majority of it is just bogus," he says. "But having said that, I believe it does occur that people actually tap into a spirit realm of sorts. I would argue that the intelligences these people have contacted are demonic."

Is It Dangerous?

While Christian experts may disagree on whether or not psychic phenomenon is real, they agree that getting involved is dangerous.

"Absolutely, whether there's demonic power or not," insists Gretchen Passantino, codirector of Answers in Action (www.answers.org), a California-based Christian apologetics ministry. "The first danger is that you're disobeying God, and in doing that you take yourself outside God's will for your life. Secondly, even if you don't want to believe it, you can be subtly drawn into it emotionally, spiritually, and psychologically."

Passantino gives an example from a Christian obstetrician who specializes in fertility problems. A Christian patient was anxious about her inability to conceive a child. A friend urged her to seek psychic advice. Even though the Christian knew it was wrong, her friend convinced her.

The psychic told her, "The good news is that you're pregnant right now, but the bad news is that your baby will never be born alive. The good news is that you'll have other healthy children."

The girl was devastated and went to the doctor to see if she was pregnant. She was. And even though everything was fine with the pregnancy the girl was so worried about the prediction that she had an abortion, fulfilling the prophecy by her own action.

Howell agrees that dabbling in occult phenomenon poses a danger for Christians, even if there are no demons involved.

"The danger is that it pulls you away from the true and living God and from his Word," Howell explains.

What Can We Do?

Interest in occult phenomena may be an opportunity for the church to reach out.

Howell says, "Surveys have shown that there's a great spiritual hunger in America. The problem is that the place where they should be looking—the church—is not where they're looking. Many times it's because we've turned them off. But there's a real desire out there, and the church can capitalize on it."

Howell agrees, "If people are open enough to the possibility that there is a realm they can't see, it may be something we can address as a church: You want to know what the future holds? God has told us everything we need to know about the future, and you can have hope in the future if you do things God's way."

Passantino explains, "People are attracted to fortune tellers and psychics because they're looking for someone with more power, more information, and more control, someone to tell me that my fears are unwarranted.

"In order to attract someone in the first place, you need to address their 'felt needs'—otherwise they don't care what you have to offer. There's nothing wrong with attracting people to the gospel by addressing felt needs, but if we don't give them the full gospel message, we're not addressing their real needs. Those needs can be met in a personal relationship with Jesus Christ, in a Bible-believing church of Christians who are committed to each other in accountability with love and mutual support."

The CIA Psychic Spy Experiment Was Unsuccessful

Michael White

For just over two decades, the U.S. government's intelligence agencies (the CIA and others) spent several million dollars funding remote-viewing research to discover whether ESP could be used as a spy tool. This was a tiny sum compared to other common intelligence expenditures and could have paid off in major ways if the research was successful. But after twenty-two years, the government decided to end its funding for the research. The government's conclusions were not that ESP did not work, but that it was not a practical tool despite many apparent astonishing remote-viewing successes.

But were the program's successes as impressive as they seemed? The program was operated jointly by a private research organization (Stanford Research Institute) and government agencies. Many scientists felt that the program was not operated as carefully as it should have been to be considered successful.

In the following article the author, Michael White, describes some of the problems he saw with the remote-viewing program. White has written many books and articles on science topics.

The Russians appear to have been the first off the mark with research into remote viewing and the uses of mental powers for military purposes. Some claim that research began in the 1920s and continued until the Berlin wall came down and communism crumbled. However, there is plenty of the usual hyperbole surrounding accounts of anything to do with military use of telepathic energies. A journalist with the magazine *Encounters* . . . stated: "First developed in the Soviet Union and then adopted by the West, psi makes some use of the ninety percent of the human brain that is normally left unused."

But even if we ignore such bland statements unsupported by any form of evidence, it is certainly true the Russians and the other major powers have been very interested in the possible practical application of psi since at least the 1940s, and despite the collapse of communism, there are almost certainly research establishments still investigating its use for military purposes. And why not? It makes perfect sense to study such things. Compared to the development of conventional weapons, the money spent on research into the paranormal would be almost insignificant, perhaps a few million dollars. Yet, if a mysterious form of telepathic power could be isolated and controlled, it would be one of the most effective weapons any nation could wish for.

Some claim that such powers have been used; but even

the most enthusiastic supporter of such ideas as psi admit that, at best, the application of these powers is inefficient and produces only patchy results.

The most popular use for mental powers by the military is as an aid for spying, and many people formerly involved with psi espionage have come forward in recent years. Some are still bound by security to keep sensitive material to themselves, but others, such as those who worked for the KGB and other Communist Bloc agencies, have been more forthcoming. As well as this source, information about the fascination with parapsychology in former Warsaw Pact countries has been known about since the 1960s, from investigators and research groups in the West, some of whom gathered first-hand experience by clandestine means during the cold war. According to some authorities, these sources alerted the Pentagon to the potential of research into psi powers. . . .

The United States and Psychic Spies

The western powers have been just as keen as the Russians to attempt to exploit any possible practical use for psi powers. In a 1992 Symposium on UFO Research, U.S. Major General Albert N. Strubblebine III chaired a seminar on remote viewing (RV) in which for the first time a high-ranking military official revealed the degree to which the U.S. government had used RV for military purposes.

Stubblebine himself headed a research group called Psi Tech, which was set up by two respected physicists, Hal Puthoff and Russell Targ at Stanford Research Institute in California, and jointly funded by the CIA and the U.S. Navy. At the talk, he claimed RV training took about one year and that selected individuals with appropriate discipline and commitment could do amazing things using the power of their minds. "Time is no object," he claimed. "I can go past, I can go present, I can go future. It is independent of location so I can go anywhere on earth. . . . I can access information at any location I choose." He then went on to describe how in 1991 his group had helped a large American corporation assess the effect of the Gulf War on the price of oil. His group came up with an answer by, he claimed, "looking inside Saddam Hussein's head."

To the dispassionate observer, there are many problems with this account. We can assume that such a group was established, but the successes they claim to have achieved are highly dubious. The overriding reason for this is that if such a group had been able to truly "go past, present, or future and any location on earth," there would be no need for any conventional spies—the U.S. government would know everything there was to know about any foreign power. In fact, such a group could easily have become billionaires and now rule the world!

We must assume that Major General Stubblebine III is, like many of us, prone to hyperbole and exaggeration. Caught up in the enthusiasm of his delivery, he must have failed to add caveats to his claims, not least of which is the fact that even the most successful remote viewers are often vague, get things wrong as often as they get things right, and are unable to give precise details except on extremely rare occasions.

The second point concerns Stubblebine's story of his involvement in Gulf War espionage. This is unconvincing on two counts. First, when a corporation funds a project, there is pressure on those employed—in this case, the remote viewers—to come up with something, anything, that might justify a check. This understandably casts everything they do in a suspicious light. But the second and far more important issue comes from the simple fact that anyone with any awareness of world affairs and global finances would be able to produce a coherent report detailing the effects of the

Gulf War on global economics. You certainly don't need to have psi powers to do that, and one of the last people to be of help would have been Saddam Hussein.

Suspicious Claims

Yet, beyond all this, in order to validate or refute this research we must look at the work of the two men who started the project, Hal Puthoff and Russell Targ. According to their own accounts, they conducted over a hundred RV experiments during the late 1970s and claim to have achieved remarkable results. In at least one set of experiments, they described a remote viewer who was able to find precisely a location not simply when a "sender" was there, but before the site was even chosen.

To the scientist, this alone would imply that something suspicious was going on with their procedure—that there must be a security leak somewhere. But putting this aside, other researchers have tried unsuccessfully to duplicate Puthoff and Targ's results. The most thorough and well-publicized of these was a set of experiments conducted by two other physicists, David Marks and Robert Kammann. They found that their subjects produced results no better than would be expected from chance or simple guesswork.

In a book the pair wrote in 1980 entitled *Psychology of the Psychic*, Marks and Kammann described their experiments, how they then contacted Puthoff and Targ to request access to their data, and how, to their amazement, their request was refused.

To deny other scientists access to one's work is almost unheard of, and immediately sets alarm bells ringing in the ears of other researchers trying to verify results. Consequently, Puthoff and Targ's refusal to release their data gave Marks and Kammann renewed enthusiasm to track down what could be happening in RV experiments.

After extensive investigation they came to the conclusion that in all the tests Puthoff and Targ performed, the remote viewer was either totally inaccurate or, when they had succeeded, they had been provided with subliminal cues or unconscious hints by those involved in the experiment. By matching the transcripts of the conversation between the viewer, the "sender," and the experimenters, Marks and Kammann showed how these clues are picked up.

In *Psychology of the Psychic*, they present many examples of how this can be done. Suppose a viewer is told that he will be required to identify three locations: 1, 2, and 3. The viewer is told that one location is a building, another is an open area, a third is a road, but they have no idea of the order in which they will come during the tests. However, in the transcript of the dialogue, there are a series of cues the experienced viewer can use. For example, the experimenter says before one of the tests: "Third time lucky." During another of the three, he says "Okay, take it slowly, we've got a long day ahead of us." With these hints, the viewer knows which site is 1, 2, or 3.

After persisting for five years and facing renewed requests from others in the field, Puthoff and Targ did eventually publish their findings, in 1985. Upon detailed analysis of these documents, independent investigators found that there were many cues given in their transcripts, particularly during the most successful remote viewing tests.

Other researchers have conducted their own investigations similar to the work of Marks and Kammann and have obtained concurring results. In a paper published in *Nature* in 1986, coauthored by Dr. Marks and an independent colleague, Dr. C. Scott, the researchers came to the scathing conclusion that "remote viewing has not been demonstrated in the experiments conducted by Puthoff and Targ, only the repeated failure of investigators to remove sensory cues."

ESP Research Does Not Follow the Rules of Science

James E. Alcock

Why do so few scientists take ESP and related phenomena seriously? Only a small number of scientists study ESP, and only a few more accept the results of ESP research as being significant. Perhaps, says James E. Alcock, the author of this article, it is because ESP research does not follow the usual rules of science. A major problem, Alcock says, is that parapsychologists—those who study such things as ESP—seem to consider all of their results, even negative ones, as proof of ESP's existence.

Alcock uses several terms that may be unfamiliar to you. Here are explanations of some of them. "Remote viewing" is a type of ESP in which a person uses mental energy alone to see something out of sight—in another room, another city, or even another country. "Psi-missing" is when the results of an experiment are significantly below normal chance; for example, a person may not get one guess correct in one hun-

Excerpted from *Science and Supernature: A Critical Appraisal of Parapsychology*, by James E. Alcock (Buffalo, NY: Prometheus Books, 1990). Copyright © 1990 by James E. Alcock. Reprinted with permission.

dred tosses of a coin. This would be extremely unusual and, say some parapsychologists, a kind of backward proof of ESP. The "decline effect" is when a person's ability to demonstrate ESP lessens over the course of an experiment or series of experiments. "Experimenter effect" is when an action by the experimenter—the researcher—affects the experiment. For example, the experimenter may unconsciously say or do something when a target picture appears, giving the remote viewer a clue. "REG" stands for "random event generator." This is a machine used in ESP experiments to randomly cause certain things to happen. For instance, it randomly changes the number of balls that fall into a chute when a lever is pushed, or it randomly selects a picture to appear on a computer screen. ESP is tested with a REG by having the "receiver" guess how many balls will fall into the chute or which picture will appear on the screen.

James E. Alcock is a psychologist and professor at Glendon College in Toronto and the author of many articles and books that challenge claims of the paranormal.

It is curious that, in this age of unprecedented literacy and unceasing scientific and technological progress, many people are prepared to accept that spoons can be bent by the power of the mind alone, that disease can be cured by the laying on of hands, that water can be located by means of a forked willow stick, or that the mind can influence the decay of radioactive substances. It is even more curious when such claims are put forth and defended by people trained in the ways of science.

Most of my readers, I would imagine, have little difficulty dismissing popular occult beliefs in astrology, palmistry, the tarot, or biorhythms. However, those same readers may not be nearly so cavalier about disregarding such supposed "paranormal" (also synonymously referred to as "parapsychological" or "psi") phenomena as extrasensory perception ("ESP") or psychokinesis ("PK"). ESP refers to the supposed ability to obtain knowledge of a target object or of another person's mental activity in the absence of sensory contact, and PK is the putative ability of the mind to influence matter directly. Belief in such phenomena is actually very widespread, not only among members of the general public but also among university students.

Such belief is no doubt tied, at least in part, to the fact that many people, perhaps even most, have from time to time had direct personal experiences that seemed to be "telepathic" or "precognitive" or "psychokinetic." Indeed, a number of surveys have found personal experience to be the major reason given by respondents for their belief in paranormal phenomena. This is not surprising: Given their often powerful emotional impact, combined with a lack of understanding about the myriad "normal" ways in which these experiences can come about, it is easy to ascribe paranormal explanations to odd experiences that one cannot readily explain otherwise. . . .

Do Scholars Take ESP Seriously?

How do members of academia view claims about psi? In one survey of humanities and science professors at two large universities, only about one-third of the respondents indicated believing in paranormal phenomena; there was no clear difference between representatives of the sciences and the humanities. This is consistent with the results of a smaller survey conducted at two other Canadian universities. Yet, . . . a much larger survey of professors at 120 colleges and universities in the United States . . . found that 73 percent of the respondents from the humanities, arts, and education indicated they believed ESP to be either an established fact or a likely possibility, whereas only 55 percent of the respondents from the natural sciences and 34 percent of the psychologists did likewise. Whether the differences between the results of the two surveys reflect differences in the questions asked or differences in the groups sampled (the former study was limited to respondents from two large and prestigious universities) is not clear. . . .

Although all of this might suggest that parapsychology is a serious and professional research discipline that is viewed with respect within university settings, at best parapsychology struggles to maintain a toehold at the fringes of academia; mainstream science continues virtually to ignore its subject matter or even to reject and ridicule it. One finds no mention of psi phenomena in textbooks of physics or chemistry or biology. Lecturers do not address the paranormal in undergraduate or graduate science programs. Psychology students are rarely taught anything about the subject. Parapsychological research papers are only very infrequently published in the journals of "normal" science, and parapsychologists have criticized leading scientific publications, such as *Science,* the *American Journal of Physics,* and *American Psychologist,* for suppressing the dissemination of parapsychological research findings. Funds for parapsychological research are usually generated within parapsychology itself or come from private donors; the agencies that fund normal science turn a blind, or even hostile, eye toward parapsychological research proposals. The United States government, however, has provided multi-million-dollar support for psi research into remote viewing at [Stanford Research Institute] International in California.

What accounts for the disparity between what would seem to be a substantial degree of professionalism in parapsychology on the one hand, and the continuing relegation of parapsychology to the fringes of science on the other? For one thing, parapsychology continually encounters opposition from mainstream psychology; psychologists appear to constitute the most skeptical group concerning whether psi is likely to exist. Second, people who may serve as the "gate-keepers" of science, in that they are very influential in determining what is and is not the proper subject matter of science, are skeptical about psi. A recent survey of "elite" scientists (Council members and selected section committee members of the American Association for the Advancement of Science) revealed the highest level of skepticism regarding ESP of any group surveyed in the past 20 years: Fewer than 4 percent of the 339 respondents . . . viewed ESP as scientifically established. (However, another 25 percent considered it to be a likely possibility. . . .) Fifty percent considered ESP to be impossible or a remote possibility.

In [one] view, this negativity is based on the threat that paranormal phenomena, were they to exist, would pose to the prevailing scientific worldview. A rather different viewpoint . . . is that parapsychology, over its century or so of existence as an empirical research endeavor, has simply failed to produce evidence worthy of scientific status. Of course *both* these views could be correct. . . .

Does ESP Follow the Rules of Science?

There are a number of principles in parapsychology that can be used to explain away failures to find empirical support for a hypothesis, thus creating a situation of unfalsifiability:

1. Perhaps the subject did significantly worse than expected by chance. If so, this may be taken as evidence of psi, because it seems to be *psi-missing*, something that occurs so often that it is now taken to be a manifestation of psi.

2. If outstanding subjects subsequently lose their psi ability, or if subjects do more poorly toward the end of a session

or of a series of trials, this is labeled the *decline affect*. Rather than being taken as a possible consequence of either statistical regression or the tightening up of controls (when that has occurred), the decline effect often takes on the power of an explanation, because it has come to be viewed as a property of psi. For example, the decline effect in one experiment was interpreted as a "sign of psi" that was taken to strengthen the claim of a genuine psi effect.

3. In a related vein, [researcher Gertrude] Schmeidler reports that PK effects are often strongest just *after* a session has terminated or during a subject's rest period. Rather than ignoring data accumulated after the session is over, this is taken to reflect another psi phenomenon, and has been given two names—the "linger effect" and the "release of effort effect." If this is to be taken seriously, then all researchers should report not only the presence of such an effect, but its absence as well: were this done, the frequency of the effect may well turn out to be within the bounds of normal statistical expectation.

The "Experimenter Effect"

4. Some parapsychologists seem consistently to obtain the results they desire whereas others are unable to find significant departures from chance. The failure of one researcher to obtain significant results using the same procedure that yielded significant results for another researcher, rather than being taken as a failure to replicate or as a hint that extraneous variables may be producing artifactual results, is often interpreted in terms of the *experimenter effect*. This effect is so common in psi research that it has even been described by one parapsychologist as parapsychology's one and only finding. To *describe* the fact that two researchers obtained different results by calling it an experimenter effect is quite appropriate. After all, the experimenter effect as such is by

no means unique to parapsychology, and a great deal has been written on the subject with regard to research in psychology and other domains. However, in psi research the term is all too often used more as an *explanation* than as a description, and that is because it is considered that the effect may result not only from experimenter error (in that one experimenter may be more successful in obtaining psi effects than another because he unwittingly allows more artifacts to contaminate his procedure), or from differences in personalities (in that some experimenters may put their subjects into a more comfortable and psi-conductive frame of mind than others), but also from the psi influence of the experimenter himself. If psi exists, of course, it would only make sense that the experimenter, who naturally wants his experiment to succeed, might unknowingly bring his psi influence to bear, whereas a skeptical or neutral experimenter might not use psi at all, or might use it to prevent the appearance of a subject psi effect. This whole problem leads [John A.] Palmer to describe the experimenter effect as the most important challenge facing parapsychology today. It is hard to imagine scientific inquiry of any sort if the results of the investigation are determined by the psychic influence of the investigator.

The experimenter effect (or the experimenter psi version of it) provides a powerful method for undermining failures to replicate, and is sometimes resorted to for just that purpose. For example, when [Susan] Blackmore, a devoted parapsychologist for many years, found herself becoming increasingly skeptical about psi as a consequence of her inability to produce experimental evidence for it, she noted that "many parapsychologists suggested that the reason I didn't get results was quite simple—*me*. Perhaps I did not sufficiently believe in the possibility of psi."

In summary, it is the way such "effects" are used—and not,

in principle, the research procedures—that vitiates the scientific respectability of parapsychology, for they make the psi hypothesis unfalsifiable by providing ways to explain away null results and nonreplications. These descriptive terms have mistakenly come to be taken as properties of psi, which leads to the circularity of explaining an observation by means of the label given to it. Moreover, as important properties of psi, their *non-appearance* in a psi experiment should weigh against any conclusion that psi has occurred; this never happens in the parapsychological literature.

All Things Are Possible?

Another aspect of parapsychology that makes critics uncomfortable is what seems to be almost an "anything goes" attitude, with no speculation seeming too wild. . . . Studies have been done that claim to show that subjects can exercise an influence backward in time ("retroactive PK") so as to affect the choice of stimulus materials preselected for the study in which they are participating. This also means, of course, that the present is possibly being influenced by future events. A "checker effect" has also been postulated, in which ESP scores may be retroactively and psychokinetically influenced by the individual who checks or analyzes the data. [Helmut] Schmidt reported that cockroaches were able to influence a random-event generator in such a way as to cause them to be shocked *more* often than would be expected by chance. He suggested that perhaps his own psi, fueled by his dislike of cockroaches, accounted for the increase, rather than a decrease, in shocks.

Not only can psi apparently transcend temporal boundaries; it also seems that no effort, no training, and no particular knowledge are required to use it. Indeed, modern PK studies appear to indicate that psi is an *unconscious* process, but a goal-oriented one in that it helps the individual attain desired objectives: Success in a PK experiment does not require knowing anything about the target, or even knowing that one is in a PK study. Thus, psi appears to operate very much like wishful thinking. For example, going back to [a 1989 study conducted by] Schmidt . . . all that was needed, it seems, was for one subject to *wish* for a particular light to come on and it would light up statistically more frequently than the others. (Of course, when subjects do score above chance, neither they nor anyone else can say which hits were brought about by psi and which were the consequence of chance.)

Lack of Constraints

The fact that no physical variable has ever been shown to influence the scoring rate in psi experiments, combined with the apparent total lack of constraints on the conditions under which psi can be manifested (whether forward in time, backward in time, across thousands of miles, between humans and objects, between humans and animals, or even between animals and objects), serves to weaken the a priori likelihood that psi, as any source of force or ability, exists. After all, most psi experiments are very similar, in that all that is typically done is to examine two sets of numbers, representing targets and responses in an ESP experiment or outcomes and aims in a PK experiment, for evidence of a nonchance association. It may simply be that the enterprise of parapsychology generates, from time to time, significant statistical deviations—be they the result of artifact, selective reporting, or whatever—which are then independent of the research hypothesis, so that no matter what the researcher is examining—the effects of healing on fungus, PK with cockroaches, ESP across a continent, or retroactive psi effects—the likelihood of obtaining significant deviations remains the same. (For example, if an REG [random event generator] produces an excess of 4s on a short-term basis, and if the procedure allows subjects to tap into this, then it should make no difference in principle whether the targets are generated on-line or were recorded a week earlier: If the subject aims for more 4s, he will obtain them.) Difficulty in replication by other researchers using their own equipment or slightly different procedures would, of course, follow from such a state of affairs, as would the experimenter effect.

This psi-as-artifact notion is not offered as an empirically testable hypothesis. I only mean to show that the lack of constraints on the appearance of psi undermines rather than strengthens its credibility. It would be hard enough to accept that a philosopher's stone can turn base metals into gold, as alchemists believed. It would be harder still to believe that it can turn *anything* into gold and that anyone can use it without any training.

Epilogue: Analyzing the Evidence

As a college psychology major, Susan Blackmore was intrigued by the suggestive evidence favoring ESP. She became a parapsychologist and devoted several years to studying ESP and other paranormal phenomena. However, she became frustrated, never able to find conclusive evidence of ESP. She developed alternate theories and experimented more, but still didn't find what she hoped to. Eventually, she abandoned her pro-ESP stance. Dean Radin also studied psychology in college and became a parapsychologist. But Radin was more fortunate in the research he undertook. He believes the results of his experiments, which were designed to test the ability of the human mind to affect events, prove that ESP is real.

So who is right about ESP—Blackmore or Radin? Even scientists who have studied the subject for many years are not in agreement. However, we can begin to shape our belief about ESP by critically examining the evidence provided by experts and by those who claim to experience ESP. Each article in this book provides various kinds of evidence and arguments in favor of the author's point of view about ESP. Some articles directly contradict others. It is the reader's job to decide which articles present a truthful and reasonable case for—or against—ESP. This can be determined by reading the article critically. This does not mean that the reader criticizes, or says negative things, about an article. It means that he or she analyzes and evaluates what the author says. This chapter describes a critical reading technique and practices using it to evaluate the articles in this book.

The Author

In deciding whether an article is good support for or against ESP, it can be helpful to learn about the author. Consider whether the author has any special qualifications for writing about the subject. For example, an article supporting ESP that was written by a scientist who has conducted ESP experiments should be taken more seriously than an article written by a telephone psychic. In this book, the editor has provided at least a small amount of information about each author. Use this information to start forming your opinion about the information in the article.

Hypothetical Reasoning

Despite whether you know anything about the author, you can evaluate an article on its own merits by using hypothetical reasoning. This is a scientific method for determining whether something makes sense, whether an author has made a reasonable case for his or her claims. For example, the author of the first article in this book claims that a man named Ted Serios is a psychic photographer—that is, he can make photographs appear on film by using his mental powers. You can use hypothetical reasoning to decide whether the author has made a reasonable argument supporting the claim. (Keep in mind that hypothetical reasoning will not necessarily prove that the author's claims are true, only that she has or has not made a reasonable case for her claims. By determining this, you know whether her arguments are worth considering when you are deciding whether ESP is real.)

To use hypothetical reasoning to analyze an article, use these five steps:

1. State the author's claim (the hypothesis).
2. Gather the author's evidence supporting the claim.
3. Examine the author's evidence.

4. Consider alternative hypotheses, or explanations, for the evidence.

5. Draw a conclusion about the author's claim.

Using hypothetical reasoning to examine several articles on ESP can give you a better perspective on the topic. You will begin to discern the difference between strong and weak evidence and to see which point of view has the most—or the best—evidence supporting it.

In the following sections, we are going to use hypothetical reasoning to critically examine some of the articles in this book. You can practice applying the method to other articles.

1. State the Author's Claim (the Hypothesis)

A hypothesis is a factual statement that can be tested to determine the likelihood of its truth. In other words, it is not merely someone's opinion; by testing it we can determine whether it is true or false. To evaluate an article critically, start by stating the author's claim. This will be the hypothesis you are going to test as you critically examine the article. The author may make several claims. To simplify, we will state one claim for each article.

In the table below, four hypothesis spaces have been left empty. After reading the directions below, write a clear, specific, and provable hypothesis for each of these four articles.

Author	Hypothesis
Pauline Oehler	Ted Serios is a psychic photographer.
Sheila Ostrander and Lynn Schroeder	Russian psychics are real.
D. Scott Rogo	Animals have ESP.
Mary Roach	
Jim Schnabel	

Author	Hypothesis
Dean Radin	Scientists have proven ESP in the laboratory.
James Randi	Ted Serios is a fraud.
Massimo Polidoro	
Ray Hyman	
Doug Trouten	Christians should stay away from ESP.
Michael White	The CIA psychic experiment was unsuccessful.
James E. Alcock	Those who study ESP do not follow the rules of science.

One important thing to remember when you write a hypothesis is that it should be a factual statement that is clear, specific, and provable. Look at the second hypothesis in the table above: "Russian psychics are real." This statement is quite general. It is better to make the hypothesis more specific. The article by Ostrander and Schroeder focuses specifically on the telekinetic abilities of one psychic, Nelya Mikhailova. So a better hypothesis would be this:

Sheila Ostrander and Lynn Schroeder	Scientists proved the telekinetic ability of Nelya Mikhailova.

Are there other hypotheses in the above table that you could make more specific?

Note that not every article has a provable hypothesis. If an article is purely a writer's opinion, you may not be able to state a provable hypothesis. Likewise, some authors avoid stating any clear claim. Many reporters remain as objective as possible, simply reporting what others say. You may not be able to write a provable hypothesis for such an article. For example, look at the hypothesis stated in the table for the article by Doug Trouten: "Christians should stay away from ESP." This statement would be difficult to prove because it is essentially an opinion. We need to state a hypothesis that can be proven true or false. The author also discusses these topics in the article: ESP may be demonic, and fooling around with ESP may be disobedience to God. But the author merely reports what other people say about these topics; he does not state a claim of his own. Putting all of the ideas in the article together, we get the idea that the author is not in favor of Christians having anything to do with ESP, but it is hard to state a provable claim.

2. Gather the Author's Evidence Supporting the Claim

Once you have a hypothesis, you must gather the evidence the author uses to support that hypothesis. The evidence is everything the author uses to prove that his or her claim is true. Sometimes an individual sentence is a piece of evidence; at other times a string of paragraphs or a section of the article is a piece of evidence. Let's look at the first article in chapter 1 to see what kinds of evidence Pauline Oehler uses to support her claim that Ted Serios is a psychic photographer:

1. The author and other people are eyewitnesses to Serios's feats.
2. Serios has produced photos of places he has never visited or seen.
3. Serios has produced his photos using cameras belonging to the author and others; he has had no chance to prepare these cameras in any way.
4. The cameras involved have had factory-sealed film packs; Serios could not have fooled with them.
5. Serios had no opportunity to dispose of secret equipment before he was carefully searched.
6. Serios uses a cardboard cylinder, but it was examined and found to be innocent.

7. Some photos are ambiguous, but even they "seem proof of a paranormal occurrence."
8. A Polaroid Corporation vice president determined that it would be extraordinarily difficult for Serios to tamper with the film.
9. Serios is not a "sleight-of-hand artist."
10. If Serios had secreted a small negative, it would not have printed properly.

3. Examine the Evidence the Author Uses to Support the Claim

An author might use many types of evidence to support his or her claims. It is important to recognize different types of evidence and to evaluate whether they actually support the author's claims. Pauline Oehler's main form of evidence is statements of fact. She also uses statements of opinion (item 7), eyewitness testimony (item 1), and expert testimonial (item 8).

Statements of fact (items 2, 3, 4, 5, 6, 9, and 10). A statement of fact presents verifiable information—that is, it can be proven to be true (or false). "Serios has produced photos of places he has never visited or seen" (item 2), is a statement of fact. The author states this as a fact, and it is a statement that is provable by investigation—we can take Serios's word for it that he has never visited or seen the places he has photographed, we can give him a lie detector test, or we can investigate his past to discover whether he has ever been to these places.

Ideally, the author should tell us the source of any statement of fact so that we can confirm it; she should tell us how she knows Serios has never been to these places. But many authors simply expect the reader to take their word for it. Be careful about accepting facts just because the author states them. Look for corroborating evidence (evidence that helps confirm their truth). For example, item 8, the Polaroid Corporation vice president's statement, helps verify item 4, that Serios could not have tampered with the film pack.

Which of Oehler's statements of fact cannot be easily verified?

Statements of opinion (item 7). A statement of opinion cannot be proven true or false—it is simply what someone believes. (Statements of opinion often are based on or contain factual statements that can be verified. For example, "I think you are angry" is a statement of opinion, but it can be verified when your face turns red and you hit me in the nose.)

Whether you accept a statement of opinion as good supporting evidence depends on the nature of the opinion and what you think of the person giving it. For instance, if your history teacher says, "Peace in the Middle East will not happen for a very long time," you may accept that as evidence because you respect that teacher's knowledge about world events. But if the same teacher tells you, "Fashion models will be wearing white socks with their black trousers next year," you may be less inclined to take this opinion seriously unless the teacher clearly keeps up with the latest fashion trends.

What do you think—is item 7 good evidence for Pauline Oehler's hypothesis?

Eyewitness testimony (item 1). Oehler is not only the author of this article, she is also an eyewitness to the events she describes. Eyewitness testimony is an interesting paradox. On one hand, who can better describe events than those who actually see them? On the other, eyewitnesses frequently get things wrong.

Perhaps you know about the eyewitness experiment in which a group of people is sitting in a classroom listening to a lecture or doing some other activity. Suddenly, the classroom door bursts open and a stranger enters. The stranger may "rob" one of the witnesses or do something else dramatic. Then the stranger leaves.

A few moments later, the instructor asks the students to tell what they witnessed. Invariably, different students remember different things. One remembers that the stranger was of average height and weight; another remembers that he was thin or heavy. One remembers that he had red hair; another remembers that a hood covered the stranger's head. One remembers that he was carrying a weapon; another remembers that his hands were empty. And so on. When something unexpected happens, especially when it happens quickly or when it evinces great emotion, the mind is not prepared to remember details. Even when the event is expected (as when Oehler expected Serios to produce psychic photographs), the witness can see things differently than what actually happened. In fact, many times eyewitnesses see exactly what they expected to see, even if that is not quite accurate.

For these reasons, independent corroborating witnesses can be very important. When investigating a criminal case, police officers often look for two or three people who saw the event and have not spoken with each other so that their accounts have not been influenced by anyone else's version. Other people witnessed Serios produce his psychic photographs, but note that in this article, we only get Oehler's account of what went on. She does not provide us with testimony from the other witnesses, she merely states that they were present.

People in certain occupations are trained to observe events very meticulously, and they are assumed to be better eyewitnesses than the average person. Police officers and airplane pilots are two examples, but even these people can be fooled.

Expert testimony (item 8). Many writers support their claims with testimony from an expert or a celebrity. A lot of television ads do this. You have probably seen the GAP commercials in which popular singers sing while wearing their GAP jeans, and you likely have seen medicine commercials in which doctors tell the benefits of that product. Advertisers know that many people are influenced when a celebrity or an expert says something is true. Article writers know this as well.

Celebrity testimony usually does not have much value as evidence: If a celebrity wears a certain brand of jeans, does it mean the jeans are good quality? No. What it really means is that the celebrity's agent got the celebrity a certain amount of money to say the jeans are good.

However, some expert testimony can provide valuable evidence. In the Oehler article, the Polaroid Corporation vice president's testimony is very valuable. He has expert knowledge about Polaroid film, so what he says about Serios being unable, without great difficulty, to tamper with the film is important.

That is the key to expert testimony: The expert must be an expert on the topic under consideration, and the author must provide enough information so that you can judge whether this person is qualified to provide valuable information.

4. Consider Alternative Hypotheses (Explanations for the Evidence)

Once you have examined the types of evidence the author has provided and considered how valuable the evidence is in supporting the author's claims, consider whether the author has presented other possible explanations. If the author considers only one explanation for the evidence, he or she may be presenting a biased, or one-sided, view or may not have fully considered the issue.

For ESP investigations, the most common alternative explanations are coincidence and fraud. Coincidence is not relevant here; it is worth considering in cases where, for example, a psychic appears to read minds or causes an object to move. The author does consider fraud, but she dismisses this explanation. It is your job to decide if the reasons she gives for rejecting this possible explanation are valid.

5. Draw a Conclusion About the Author's Claim

After considering the evidence and alternative explanations, it is time to make a judgment, to decide whether the hypothesis makes sense. You can tally up the evidence that does and does not support the hypothesis and see how many pros and cons you have. But that is really too simple. You will have to give more weight to some evidence than to others. For instance, most of the evidence in Oehler's article are statements of fact, much of which is hard to verify, so you have to decide whether the author's account is accurate. What do you think—does Oehler adequately support the claim that Ted Serios psychically produces photographs? What most convinces you?

Exploring Further

Let's examine another article using hypothetical reasoning. Take a look at James Randi's article, "Ted Serios Is a Fraud." Perhaps the first thing to notice is that Randi comes to this subject with a bias against it. Randi is a member of the Committee for the Scientific Investigation of Claims of the Paranormal (CSICOP) and a longtime skeptic of anything paranormal. Pauline Oehler, too, had a preexisting bias: She was a member of the Illinois Society for Psychical Research, a pro-paranormal organization. Thus, as we read either article, we must decide whether the author puts aside his or her bias and treats the subject as objectively as possible.

Now let's review Randi's article using the steps for hypothetical reasoning.

1. State a Hypothesis
Ted Serios is a fraud.

2. Gather the Author's Evidence

1. Ted Serios is "an ex-bellboy turned 'psychic.'"
2. Dr. Jule Eisenbud "supported the Polaroid Corporation" for two years by "purchasing vast quantities of film and having Serios make silly pictures."
3. Serios was asked to make a picture of the submarine *Thresher*, but it looked like Queen Elizabeth. But Eisenbud says the photo worked because of wordplay with the queen's name.
4. Serios made a picture of fugitive Patty Hearst with short hair; when Hearst was captured she had long hair.
5. Randi tells us how to make a "gizmo" like Serios used and how to use it to make "psychic" photos.
6. Eisenbud suggests that if Serios is successful 10 percent of the time, it proves he is a psychic, but Randi says 10 percent is within very generous normal limits.
7. *Life* magazine published an article supporting Serios, but it left out some detrimental facts.
8. Eisenbud demonstrated "the irrationality of his kind."
9. When two photographers and a conjuring authority went to see Serios perform, Eisenbud prevented them from having an unobstructed view.
10. Security during the Serios experiments was so bad that a witness was able to switch a batch of film without Eisenbud noticing.
11. Eisenbud challenged Randi to produce the type of photos Serios produces, but with more rigid controls.
12. Serios produced photos only when he used his "gizmo."

13. Eisenbud "is not rowing with both oars in the water."

14. Persi Diaconis, an expert in conjuring and statistics, says that parapsychological research is generally "poorly designed, badly run, and inappropriately analyzed."

15. Diaconis says that "what transpired" during the Serios experiments prevents them "from being considered seriously as evidence for paranormal phenomena."

3. Examine the Evidence

In this article, Randi relies most heavily on ridicule and innuendo. He also uses statements of fact, statistics, negative association, physical evidence, and expert testimony.

Ridicule and innuendo (items 1, 2, 3, 8, and 13). Also known as name-calling, ridicule and innuendo make fun of something in order to decrease its credibility. In general, this is not useful evidence. Many times, an author uses this as a substitute for real evidence. You must read carefully to see if there is any evidence behind the ridicule.

In this article, some of Randi's statements are pure name-calling (item 11, for example) and are thus meaningless as evidence; but some are making fun of what Randi considers weak evidence on the part of Serios's supporters and have to be analyzed for significance. In item 3, for instance, Randi gives an example of the ridiculous extremes he thinks Dr. Jule Eisenbud went to in defending Serios. You will have to decide if Randi's example supports his hypothesis.

Look at the other items listed here. Which ones provide some supporting evidence for Randi's hypothesis?

Statements of fact (items 4, 7, 9, 10, and 12). Review the information about statements of fact in the section of this chapter that discusses Pauline Oehler's article. Then decide if the items listed here provide good evidence for Randi's hypothesis.

Statistics (item 6). Authors sometimes use statistics or other numerical data to support their claims or refute their opponents' claims. For example, they may state that an idea is correct because of the large number of people who believe it. When deciding whether something happened by chance or on purpose, statistics are very important. In item 6, Randi states that Eisenbud considers a 10 percent success rate to be significant, but Randi considers that to be within normal results. For something like this, it is helpful to have a source to check what would provide a normal percentage. The author sometimes provides that information.

Evaluate all numerical claims carefully. Where did the numbers come from? If they are from a survey, how old is the survey? What do the numbers really mean?

Negative association (items 8 and 14). Also called "tarring with the same brush," the term *negative association* means to mention a negative example and then associate one's opponent with it. In item 14, for example, Diaconis suggests that most parapsychology experiments are not conducted properly, and Randi then automatically puts Eisenbud's experiments into the same category. If he provides no other support for this idea, negative association is not good evidence. However, Randi has provided other support for the idea that Eisenbud's experiments with Serios were not properly controlled (item 10, for instance).

Physical evidence (item 5). Physical evidence can be used to prove or disprove a hypothesis. In police cases, physical evidence includes things like fingerprints, DNA, murder weapons, and so on. In this article, physical evidence is the photographs Ted Serios makes. Randi tells us how to make similar photographs by using a little device that is easy to make. He gives us the ammunition to evaluate the physical evidence for ourselves. If Randi's "gizmo" works, it puts Serios's photos into a questionable light.

Expert testimony (items 14 and 15). Review the information on expert testimony in the section on Oehler's article. Does Diaconis's expert testimony lend credible support to Randi's hypothesis?

4. Consider Alternative Hypotheses

Does Randi consider alternative hypotheses? Does he consider explanation for his evidence other than that Ted Serios is a fraud? Can you think of alternative hypotheses he should have considered?

5. Draw a Conclusion

You decide: Does James Randi make a good case for Ted Serios being a fraud? What evidence most influences your decision?

Other Evidence

Authors commonly use other types of evidence to support their claims. One important type of evidence is logical thinking, or logical argument. *Logic* comes from the Greek word for "reason." Logical thinking means to reason things out. (Hypothetical reasoning is a form of logical thinking.) A logical fallacy is when logical reasoning fails: You think you are reasoning logically, but you are not. For example, you might make an overgeneralization: You say, "I have never experienced ESP, therefore it does not exist." This may appear to be logical, but it is not. There are a lot of things you have not experienced that are real. For instance, you have not experienced spaceflight, the bubonic plague, or death, yet all exist.

Another kind of logical fallacy is a false analogy: You wrongly compare two things based on a common quality. Here is an example:

Honey bees make honey. Honey bees have yellow stripes.
Wasps also have yellow stripes, so wasps must make honey.

The fallacy is that honey making has nothing to do with
yellow stripes, so the argument falls apart. Here is another
example of a logical fallacy:

My dog seems to sense when I will be home from school.
My neighbor's dog also senses when he will be home from
  school.
Therefore, all dogs sense when their owners will be home
  from school.

The fallacy here is that your sample is too small. There are
millions of dogs in the world, and you know only two of
them. This is far too few to base such a broad generalization
on.

As you read, carefully examine the author's logical thinking.

Now You Do It!

Choose one article from this book that has not already been
analyzed and use hypothetical reasoning to determine if the
author's evidence supports the hypothesis. Here is a form
you can use:

Name of article_____ Author_____

1. State the author's hypothesis.

2. List the evidence.

3. Examine the evidence. For each item you have listed under number 2, state what type of evidence it is (statement of
fact, eyewitness testimony, etc.) and evaluate it: Does it appear to be valid evidence? Does it appear to support the author's hypothesis?

4. Consider alternative hypotheses. What alternative hypotheses does the author consider? Does he or she consider them fairly? If the author rejects them, does the rejection seem reasonable? Are there other alternative explanations you believe should be considered? Explain.

5. Draw a conclusion about the hypothesis. Does the author adequately support his or her claim? Do you believe the author's hypothesis stands up? Explain.

Glossary

clairaudience: "Clear hearing"; the ability to hear something not audible through the normal sense of hearing.

clairvoyance: "Clear seeing"; the ability see something or to perceive something not visible to normal eyesight; often this refers to the ability to "see" the future.

ESP: Extrasensory perception; also known as telepathy.

extrasensory perception: ESP; the ability to obtain information about objects or events without the use of the five senses of hearing, sight, smell, taste, and touch; extrasensory perception is often broken down into several types of phenomena, including clairvoyance, precognition, telekinesis, and telepathy.

Ganzfeld: "Whole field"; a form of ESP experimentation in which the receiver or the sender is placed in an environment that, as much as possible, has been cleared of all normal sensory inputs.

paranormal: "Beyond the normal"; things that cannot be explained by scientific means.

parapsychology: The study of the paranormal.

PK: Psychokinesis; another name for telekinesis; the ability to move or otherwise affect objects with mental power alone.

precognition: Perceiving or knowing something before it happens; clairvoyance.

psi: A common term for anything related to the paranormal.

psychic: 1. Descriptive term for a paranormal ability; for example, ESP. 2. A person with paranormal ability.

psychic phenomena: Occurrences, abilities, objects, and beings that cannot be explained by ordinary means.

receiver: In ESP experiments, the person who is attempting to receive messages or images by telepathy.

REG: Random-event generator; a machine that randomly (that is, without a pattern) provides a "target" for ESP receivers or remote viewers to perceive or to try to affect by mental power; the target could be an image on a television screen, a certain playing card, or balls falling into a chute, for example.

remote viewing: Using the mind to "see" something that is far away or completely obscured.

sender: In ESP experiments, the person who is attempting to send messages or images to a receiver by telepathy.

sensory deprivation: The elimination of normal sensory input by isolating, blindfolding, or using other techniques to block normal hearing, sight, smell, taste, and touch; used in ESP research to eliminate distractions that might interfere with sending and receiving messages and images by telepathy.

sixth sense: A psychic sense; a sense in addition to the normal five senses (hearing, sight, smell, taste, and touch) that allows a person to perceive or know things by mental power alone.

telekinesis: The ability to move or in some other way affect objects or living beings by mental power; also known as PK.

telepathy: Mind-to-mind communication; also known as ESP.

For Further Research

James E. Alcock, *Science and the Supernatural: A Critical Appraisal of Parapsychology.* Buffalo, NY: Prometheus, 1990.

Loyd Auerbach, *Psychic Dreaming: A Parapsychologist's Handbook.* New York: Warner Books, 1991.

Sharon Begley, "Is There Anything to It? Evidence, Please," *Newsweek*, July 8, 1996.

John Beloff, *Parapsychology: A Concise History.* New York: St. Martin's, 1993.

Richard S. Broughton, *Parapsychology: The Controversial Science.* New York: Ballantine, 1991.

Paul Chambers, *Paranormal People: The Famous, the Infamous, and the Supernatural.* London: Blandford, 1998.

Martin Ebon, *They Knew the Unknown.* New York: New American Library, 1971.

Martin Ebon, ed., *The Signet Handbook of Parapsychology.* New York: New American Library, 1978.

Hans J. Eysenck and Carl Sargent, *Explaining the Unexplained: Mysteries of the Paranormal.* London: Prion, 1993.

FATE, FATE Presents: Psychic Pets and Spirit Animals. St. Paul, MN: Llewellyn, 1997.

Steve Fishman, "Questions for the Cosmos," *New York Times Magazine*, November 26, 1989.

Michael W. Fox, "Understanding Your Pet: Those Strange Stories About Psychic Animals," *McCall's*, August 1980.

Kendrick Frazier, "Lab Experiments Demonstrate Social Transmission of Paranormal," *Skeptical Inquirer*, March 2002.

Kendrick Frazier, ed., *Science Confronts the Paranormal*. Buffalo, NY: Prometheus, 1986.

Fred M. Frohock, *Lives of the Psychics: The Shared Worlds of Science and Mysticism*. Chicago: University of Chicago Press, 2000.

Robert Gardner, *What's So Super About the Supernatural?* Brookfield, CT: Twenty-First Century Books, 1998.

Uri Geller and Guy Lyon Playfair, *The Geller Effect*. New York: Henry Holt, 1986.

Bernard Gittelson, *Intangible Evidence*. New York: Simon and Schuster/A Fireside Book, 1987.

Dale E. Graff, *Tracks in the Psychic Wilderness: An Exploration of ESP, Remote Viewing, Precognitive Dreaming, and Synchronicity*. Boston: Element Books, 1998.

Harper's, "I See Red People," December 2001.

Hans Holzer, *FATE Presents: The Psychic Side of Dreams*. St. Paul, MN: Llewellyn, 1992.

Ray Hyman, "Evaluation of the Military's Twenty-Year Program on Psychic Spying," *Skeptical Inquirer*, March/April 1996. *See also other articles and books by this author.*

Alexander Imich, ed., *Incredible Tales of the Paranormal: Documented Accounts of Poltergeist, Levitations, Phantoms, and Other Phenomena*, New York: Bramble Books, 1995.

Brian Inglis, *Natural and Supernatural: A History of the Paranormal from Earliest Times to 1914*. Dorset, UK: Prism, 1992.

H.J. Irwin, *An Introduction to Parapsychology*. 3rd ed. Jefferson, NC: McFarland, 1999.

Robert G. Jahn and Brenda J. Dunne, *Margins of Reality: The Role of Consciousness in the Physical World*. San Diego: Harcourt Brace Jovanovich, 1997.

Carl Jones, "Parents and Kids: The ESP Connection," *McCall's*, May 1989.

Paul Kurtz, ed., *A Skeptic's Handbook of Parapsychology*. Buffalo, NY: Prometheus, 1985.

Scott O. Lilienfeld, "New Analyses Raise Doubts About Replicability of ESP Findings," *Skeptical Inquirer*, November 1999.

Kenneth Miller, "Psychics: Science or Séance?" *Life*, June 1998.

David Morehouse, *Psychic Warrior: Inside the CIA's Stargate Program: The True Story of a Soldier's Espionage and Awakening*. New York: St. Martin's, 1996.

Jill Neimark, "Do the Spirits Move You?" *Psychology Today*, September/October 1996.

New Scientist, "Interview: Tales of the Paranormal," March 3, 2001.

———, "Opinion Interview: I'm Thinking . . . ," August 28, 1999.

Joe Nickell with John F. Fischer, *Mysterious Realms: Probing Paranormal, Historical, and Forensic Enigmas*. Buffalo, NY: Prometheus, 1992.

Joe Nickell, Barry Kerr, and Tom Genoni, eds., *The Outer Edge: Classic Investigations of the Paranormal*. Amherst, NY: CSICOP, 1996.

Pauline Oehler, *The Psychic Photography of Ted Serios*. Chicago: Illinois Society for Psychic Research, n.d.

Sheila Ostrander and Lynn Schroeder, *Psychic Discoveries*. New York: Marlowe & Company, 1970.

Massimo Polidoro, "Secrets of a Russian Psychic," *Skeptical Inquirer*, July/August 1997.

Benjamin Radford, "Worlds in Collision: Applying Reality to the Paranormal," *Skeptical Inquirer*, November/December 2000.

Dean Radin, *The Conscious Universe: The Scientific Truth of Psychic Phenomena*. San Francisco: HarperEdge, 1997.

Dean Radin and Colleen Rae, "Is There a Sixth Sense?" *Psychology Today*, July 2000.

Mary Roach, "A Postcard from the Twilight Zone," *Health*, July/August 1993.

D. Scott Rogo, "Psi Fear," *Omni*, September 1987.

Stephen Sawicki, "Seizure Alert," *Animals*, January 1999.

Jim Schnabel, *Remote Viewers: The Secret History of America's Psychic Spies*. New York: Dell, 1997.

Charles E. Sellier, *The Paranormal Handbook: A Comprehensive Guide to All Things Otherworldly*. Los Angeles: Roxberry Park/Lowell House, 1999.

Rupert Sheldrake, *Dogs That Know When Their Owners Are Coming Home and Other Unexplained Powers of Animals*. New York: Crown, 1999.

Skeptical Inquirer, "Science Indicators 2000: Belief in the Paranormal or Pseudoscience," January 2001.

Brad Steiger and Sherry Hansen Steiger, *More Strange Powers of Pets*. New York: Donald I. Fine, 1994.

Victor J. Stenger, *Physics and Psychics: The Search for a World Beyond the Senses*. Buffalo, NY: Prometheus, 1990.

Lisa Suhay, "Grandpa's Song," *Family Circle*, November 16, 1999.

Russell Targ and Keith Harary, *The Mind Race: Understanding and Using Psychic Abilities.* New York: Villard Books, 1984.

Doug Trouten, "Paranormal Deception," *Christian Reader,* March 2001.

Michael White, *Weird Science: An Expert Explains Ghosts, Voodoo, the UFO Conspiracy, and Other Paranormal Phenomena.* New York: Avon, 1999.

Index

156